GREAT
COMMISSION
COMPANIES

THE EMERGING ROLE OF BUSINESS IN MISSIONS

STEVE RUNDLE
AND TOM STEFFEN

InterVarsity Press
Downers Grove, Illinois

InterVarsity Press
P.O. Box 1400, DownersGrove, IL 60515-1426
World Wide Web: www.ivpress.com
E-mail: mail@ivpress.com

InterVarsity Press® is the book-publishing division of InterVarsity Christian Fellowship/USA®, a student movement active on campus at hundreds of universities, colleges and schools of nursing in the United States of America, and a member movement of the International Fellowship of Evangelical Students. For information about local and regional activities, write Public Relations Dept., InterVarsity Christian Fellowship/USA, 6400 Schroeder Rd., P.O. Box 7895, Madison, WI 53707-7895, or visit the IVCF website at <www.ivcf.org>.

All Scripture quotations, unless otherwise indicated, are taken from the Holy Bible, New International Version®. NIV®. *Copyright ©1973, 1978, 1984 by International Bible Society. Used by permission of Zondervan Publishing House. All rights reserved.*

Figures not original to this book are used with permission. See captions for sources.

Design: Cindy Kiple

Cover image: Roz Woodward/Getty Images

ISBN 0-8308-3227-0

Printed in the United States of America ∞

Library of Congress Cataloging-in-Publication Data

Rundle, Steve, 1959-

   Great commission companies: the emerging role of business in
   missions
/ Steve Rundle and Tom Steffen.
     p. cm.
Includes bibliographical references and index.
   ISBN 0-8308-3227-0 (pbk.: alk. paper)
   1. Business enterprises—Religious aspects. 2. Missions—Finance.
I. Steffen, Tom A. 1947-   II. Title.
   HF5388.R86 2003
   266—dc22

2003016150

P	17	16	15	14	13	12	11	10	9	8	7	6	5	4	3
Y	15	14	13	12	11	10	09	08	07	06	05	04			

CONTENTS

PREFACE

It is easy to understand the ambivalence toward globalization. On one hand, we enjoy the wide variety of products and services available, many of which have their origins in other parts of the world. Our lives are being enriched by an international potpourri of music, food, sports, medicine and fashion. But on the other hand, we are more concerned than ever about our job security and wages because our employers must now compete with firms from all over the world. We are also uneasy about the growing influence global financial markets are having on our government's ability to set its own domestic priorities. And finally, we are deeply troubled by the stories about human rights violations and environmental degradation by some high-profile multinational corporations.

Exactly what should be done about globalization, however, is a matter of intense debate. Some are convinced that it represents the best hope ever for economic advancement, particularly for the two to three billion people—almost half of the world's population—who continue to live in grinding poverty. Furthermore they believe that the "invisible hand" of free markets, combined with the watchful eye of activists and a scandal-hungry media, will make corporate irresponsibility unprofitable. Others are less sanguine, viewing globalization as a new form of cultural and economic imperialism, or worse, as a sinister force that not only undermines minimal standards of human decency but in fact makes poor countries even worse off.

Within this context, our book takes an expectant and relatively optimistic look at globalization because it is based on one indisputable fact: *Globalization did not catch God by surprise, nor is it out of his control.* On the contrary, we believe that globalization is a continuation of God's plan, first revealed to Abram, to bless all nations and peoples of the earth (see Gen 12:3). Moreover we believe that this redemptive plan, which is the central message of the Bible, is the intended purpose of the *whole* church, not merely those in professional ministry. Globalization is helping undo the modern dichotomy between spiritual and worldly professions, in part by bringing businesses of all sizes into countries that are in desperate spiritual and economic need. This is creating unprecedented new opportunities for Christian business professionals who desire to use their God-given skills to impact the world for Jesus Christ. In short, we believe there is a different "invisible hand" at work, the hand of Almighty God.

Globalization is changing the missions landscape in many important ways, and the increasing role of what we call Great Commission Companies (GCCs) is only part of that story. But it is a part of the story that has not received much attention from business or missions scholars and is therefore not well understood. This book is an initial step toward integrating an economic and missiological analysis of the methods, structures and results of these companies. Our recommendations and conclusions are not intended to be the final word, by any means. On the contrary, we hope this book will be the beginning of a long and fruitful discussion about how businesses can be used to bring the good news in word and deed to the neediest and least-evangelized parts of the world.

DATA AND METHODOLOGY

This book is based on five years of studying and visiting for-profit companies that have a missional purpose. Over this period we have collectively spoken to hundreds of men and women working in this context. In addition to interviewing Americans and Western Europeans, we have met with lay professionals—"kingdom professionals"—from India, China, South Korea, Singapore, Malaysia and Eastern Europe who are using their businesses to bring the healing message of the gospel to places that are difficult to reach with traditional missionary strategies. From these visits and interviews we have identified some of the principles and practices behind the most effective GCCs.

By secular standards, all the companies profiled in this book are small, with valuations typically below five million dollars and a workforce of ten to two thousand employees. However, by missions standards, they are very large companies. We deliberately chose larger companies in order to push the envelope a bit. Many people in professional ministry have been wary of mixing business and missions, and as a consequence have pursued it only halfheartedly, usually with limited success. Their lack of success then confirms their belief that business and ministry do not mix well. By contrast, we have found that large, job-creating, tax-paying, export-oriented businesses are often *more* effective because they are generally more respected in the community and able to minister in ways that are impossible for individuals or small companies. Larger companies are also more secure in countries that are hostile to Christian ministries because the cost of expelling such companies increases with its size. Put another way, the local government has more to lose by expelling a large and profitable business than it does a small, struggling, even phony enterprise.

Combining business and missions is not easy, and it creates a tension that does not exist when the activities are pursued separately. But the fact that it is difficult is not a valid reason for not trying. People need to start sharing their stories—their successes as well as failures—so that Christians can become more consistently effective and successful in this area. With that broader purpose in mind, the people profiled in this book have been exceedingly generous about sharing their time, their stories and some very private company data. For the sake of corporate and personal security, some details have been omitted or altered. With the exception of Pura Vida Coffee, the names and locations have been changed (some to fictional names, such as the country of Nearstan). Any resemblance to the name of an actual company is purely coincidental.

ACKNOWLEDGMENTS

Not long ago many people viewed the term "Christian businessman" (or woman) as an oxymoron. Thus we want to first acknowledge scholars, such as Michael Novak, Richard Chewning and R. Paul Stevens, who have tirelessly defended the biblical legitimacy of free-market economics and the positive impact Christians can have in the marketplace. In the face of much opposition, these and other Christian scholars forcefully argued that business is itself a calling, that the marketplace is a legitimate mission field and indeed is a place that *needs* Christians who will stem the corrosive economic effects of an unchecked sin nature. As a direct result of their work, the tide is now shifting, and many Christians recognize that the marketplace is a valid, honorable career choice for ministry-oriented Christians.

Integrating *crosscultural missions* into a business career is still a relatively new concept, however. In the course of our own research, there were several people who made significant contributions to this book by volunteering many hours of their valuable time to dialogue with us, read drafts or in other ways help shape our thinking. Among this group of people we would like to thank Tom Buckles, James Engel, Dave English, Paul Fitzgerald, Pete Hammond, Jerry Hogshead, C. Neal Johnson, Patrick Lai, Dwight Nordstrom, Mike Phillips, John Sage, Tom Sudyk, Sharon Swarr, Gary Taylor, John Warton, Ralph Winter, William Wood and Ted Yamamori. We are also deeply indebted to the Biola Faculty Research and Development Committee and our deans—Larry Strand and Doug Pennoyer—for their generous support. Finally, we want to thank the students at Biola who participated in various focus groups, classes and workshops. Regrettably, we have not incorporated everyone's suggestions into this book, and we take full responsibility for any errors or weaknesses that are the result.

Steve Rundle
Tom Steffen

PART ONE

PRINCIPLES OF GREAT COMMISSION COMPANIES

1
THE GOOD NEWS ABOUT GLOBALIZATION

But thanks be to God, who always leads us in triumphal procession in Christ and through us spreads everywhere the fragrance of the knowledge of him. (2 Cor 2:14)

integrate *(ĭn´tĭ-grāt´) v. 1. To make into a whole by bringing all parts together. 2. To end the segregation of and bring into common and equal membership in society.*

An employee is assaulted by a gang of thugs over the weekend, and Jeff, the founder and CEO of the company, takes the opportunity to instruct the new believer about what Christ meant when he said, "Love your enemies." By the end of the meeting they are in a quiet room asking God to bless the young men who did this. In a similar way, an entrepreneur named Patrick finds creative ways to turn seemingly mundane events at work into teaching opportunities. For example, on one occasion he uses a workplace illustration to help a Muslim employee understand the unbelievable and unnatural concept of grace. On another, he explains why the company gives away a third of its profits—through an employee-managed fund—to local charities. Business owner Jung-Hyuk believed God wanted him to move his company from South Korea to China, and five years later a quarter of his two thousand employees are following Christ. Many have taken advantage of the company-sponsored classes in computers, English, Korean, nutrition, music and dance, and some are even receiving corporate scholarships for formal pastoral training.

These are just a few examples of the increasing role businesses and the professionals who manage them are playing in the Great Commission. The specific examples were taken from companies located in Central, East and Southeast Asia, but these same things are happening everywhere, thanks in part to the phenomenon commonly called globalization. When most people talk about globalization, they are referring to the reduction in the political, social and economic barriers that once kept countries and nationalities largely separate. But there is another barrier falling—a theological one—that is having a profound effect on how the church understands and fulfills its purpose. This barrier is the unwritten "spiritual-vocational hierarchy" that has governed the way many people think about their role in Christian ministry. This hierarchy treats some vocations, specifically those higher up on the pyramid in figure 1.1, as more God-pleasing and honorable than others. According to this theology, those who are the most sincere about their commitment to Christ will get special vocational training, switch careers and become professional Christian workers supported by the donations of the rest of the church. The implication is that spiritual growth naturally leads maturing Christians to exchange their careers at the bottom end of the pyramid for those closer to the peak.

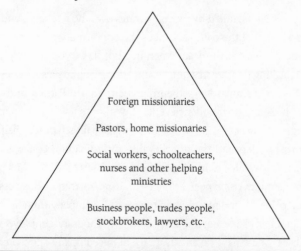

Foreign missioniaries

Pastors, home missionaries

Social workers, schoolteachers, nurses and other helping ministries

Business people, trades people, stockbrokers, lawyers, etc.

Figure 1.1. Spiritual-vocational hierarchy. Adapted from R. Paul Stevens, *The Other Six Days: Vocation, Work, and Ministry in Biblical Perspective* (Grand Rapids: Eerdmans, 1999).

The only problem with this view is that there is no biblical support for it. Professional Christian workers certainly have their place, and God does occasionlly prompt people to switch vocations, but there is nothing vocation-specific about our call to be full-time bearers of good news. As theologian R. Paul Stevens wrote in his book *The Other Six Days: Vocation, Work, and Ministry in Biblical Perspective,* "Mission is the intended occupation and pre-occupation of the whole people of God, not merely a few chosen representative or designated missionaries."[1] Our individual callings and gifts may differ, but mission is nevertheless the central purpose of the *entire* body of Christ. The perceived distinction between "good" and "better" vocations has served only to undermine the effectiveness of the church because many Christians simply resign themselves to second-class status, or worse, become completely detached from any involvement in ministry. Using an analogy of Ed Silvoso of Harvest Evangelism, the end result is something that resembles a match that has gone into overtime in soccer's World Cup:

> A handful of players, all in desperate need of rest, run all over the field while hundreds of thousands of spectators . . . watch from comfortable seats. The players are the ministers who exert most of the energy, and the spectators represent the laypeople whose participation is limited to a secondary role, mainly making the whole enterprise financially feasible.[2]

This book is for the countless Christian men and women in business who want to do more than watch the game of missions. They want to do more than dole out money to make the game financially viable; *they want to be on the playing field.* They have served on church committees, they have reflected Christ in their workplaces, they have participated in short-term missions trips, but the unmistakable message they continue to receive is that anything more requires a career change. This is a tough pill to swallow for people who are creative and resourceful by nature, and who quite frankly enjoy the business career. The purpose of this book is to show how it is not only *possible* today, but also *necessary* for business professionals—and companies owned by Christians—to become more actively involved in missions.

Our main focus will be on companies that are bringing the healing message of the gospel to the least-developed and least-evangelized parts of the world. We recognize, of course, that the Great Commission applies at home as well as abroad. Matthew 28:18-20 implies this, and Christ's final words to his disciples in Acts 1:8 remove any doubt. However, it is also true that almost 27 percent of the world's population—some 1.6 billion people—still have no idea who Jesus Christ is or why his death and resurrection matter. Furthermore, they will likely never encounter a *single* follower of Jesus, even though in some cases there is a substantial Christian population surrounding them. As we can see in figure 1.2, almost all of these so-called unreached people live in the Eastern hemisphere, with the heaviest concentrations located in Asia, the Middle East and North Africa.

The reason for these pockets of unreached people is that the gospel tends to stay within cultures and cross linguistic or cultural barriers only when a deliberate effort is made. The barriers are even more significant if reinforced by centuries of conflict and prejudice. For example, Palestinian Christians are unlikely to have much success evangelizing their Israeli neighbors, and vice versa. The same is true of a Turkish Christian trying to communicate the gospel to one of the seven distinct Kurdish people groups. All over the world, invisible walls separate people into 16,800 "people groups" and inhibit the gospel's spread. In India alone there are more than two thousand distinct people groups. While an estimated sixty-two million Indians classify themselves as Christian they represent only 6.2 percent of the population, and the majority of the people groups have never heard the gospel.[3] The same is true in China, Pakistan, Indonesia and other countries that have substantial Christian populations but are still considered largely unreached.

Adding insult to injury, roughly 90 percent of the world's poorest and most suffering people live in these same countries. (See figure 1.3.) In such parts of the world, poverty is defined not by whether a person has a home with heat, electricity and indoor plumbing, but simply by the person's ability to remain alive from one day to the next. According to the World Bank, almost a quarter of the world's population struggles on one dollar per day or less, and nearly half of the world survives on less than two dollars per day. These countries are also plagued by a long list of other problems that are closely related to poverty, such as a lower average life expectancy, higher infant mortality rates, lower literacy rates and so on.

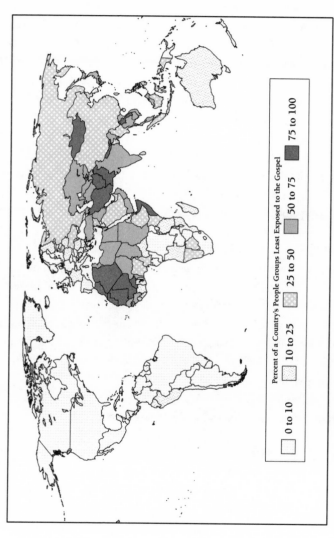

Figure 1.2. The world's most unreached people. Source: Global Mapping International. Used with permission.

Large parts of the world are suffering, unreached and off-limits to *professional* Christian workers. Frankly, most of these countries are not interested in allowing people into the country for the sole purpose of converting others to their religion. As a result, the missionary visa is quickly becoming a relic of colonialism, and professional Christian workers must find other ways to gain entry into those countries. Some gain access by providing humanitarian services, but these tend to reach only the most displaced and desperate segments of society. Business, on the other hand, has "a remarkable capacity to touch virtually every person on the face of this planet," as one observer put it.[4] Radio and television ministries have a similar potential but are limited in their ability to stimulate economies or meet physical needs. Moreover only flesh-and-blood people can build relationships and model the gospel in real-life settings. Business provides such a context for long-term holistic outreach.

This is not a book about microenterprise development. As valid as helping people start their own small businesses may be, what we are describing is a markedly different approach to economic and spiritual development. This approach borrows a page from something that most governments and economists have recognized for a long time: multinational corporations—properly motivated—can greatly assist the development process by upgrading a country's economic capabilities, contributing to its integration into the global economy and fighting against poverty and other socioeconomic problems. (Chapter three will identify the factors that enhance a company's development potential.)

Large foreign-owned companies can also have a spiritual impact that many missionaries envy for the simple reason that people spend so much more time at work than they do in traditional ministry contexts. Evangelism and discipleship can be integrated into natural workday situations rather than forced to compete with a host of after-work alternatives. Meetings with customers and suppliers become God-designed, Spirit-abetted opportunities to build relationships and have a meaningful influence in people's lives. Lunchrooms double as places where prayer, Bible study and worship can take place. Corporate profits can be used to support other ministry outside the company. The companies mentioned at the beginning of the chapter are

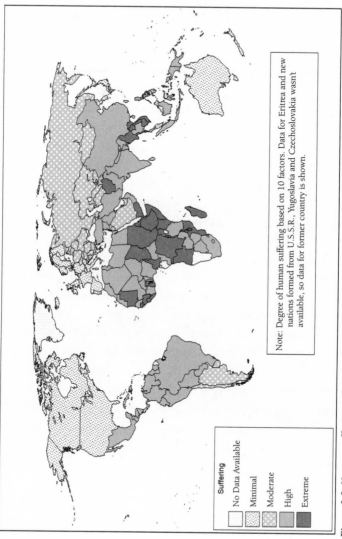

Figure 1.3. Human suffering index. Source: Global Mapping International. Used with permission.

Note: Degree of human suffering based on 10 factors. Data for Eritrea and new nations formed from U.S.S.R., Yugoslavia and Czechoslovakia wasnt available, so data for former country is shown.

Suffering

- No Data Available
- Minimal
- Moderate
- High
- Extreme

only a few examples of this. We have found that, regardless of whether they are managed by Western or non-Western Christians, large expatriate-managed companies are having a consistently significant impact for Christ in some of the least-developed and least-evangelized parts of the world.

A NEW, NOT-SO-NEW IDEA

Using business as a vehicle for missions and ministry is not new. The apostle Paul, for example, was a full-time leather worker during much of his missionary career. A study of his letters reveals that working was more than a way to support himself; it was a central part of his missionary strategy. Preaching the gospel for free added credibility to his message and served as a model for his converts to follow (see 1 Cor 9:12-18). "By working for a living, Paul set a pattern of lay witness and ministry by regular, working Christians," notes Dave English of Global Opportunities. He "made it normative for every Christian to make disciples."[5] In the Middle Ages, Christian monks integrated work and ministry by tilling fields, clearing forests and building roads, while also tending to the sick, the orphaned and the imprisoned, protecting the poor, and teaching the children. The transforming effect was significant over time. As villages and towns sprang up around the monasteries, the surrounding society incorporated many of these same social concerns.[6] Even as recently as the nineteenth century, many early Protestants such as the Moravians, the Basel Mission Society and William Carey integrated business and other secular occupations into their mission strategies.[7]

So why then does this seem so new and unfamiliar? There are at least three reasons why today's missions community has been reluctant to work closely with business. First, there is the recent but deeply entrenched belief that "work" takes time away from "ministry." The closest a person can come to integrating the two is to pursue ministry on a part-time or bivocational basis, which is usually understood to mean wearing a work hat for part of the day and a ministry hat for the other part. Never before in the history of the church has this oil-and-water perspective been so widely and uncritically accepted. Michael McLoughlin of Youth With A Mission notes with irony that once people quit their jobs to go into full-time ministry, they become isolated from the very people with whom they once had daily contact.[8]

Rather than spending forty hours per week with the people, they are now on the fringes, trying to squeeze in a Bible study here or a breakfast meeting there. Roland Allan made a similar observation in his 1930 book *The Case for the Voluntary Clergy,* when he noted that full-time, donor-supported missionaries are "constantly struggling to get close to the laity by wearing lay clothing, sharing in lay amusements and organizing lay clubs; but they never quite succeed. To get close to [people], it is necessary really to share their experience, and to share their experience is to share it by being in it, not merely to come as near to it as possible without being in it."[9]

Second is the closely related belief that a business can either serve society or make money, but not both. There is nothing new about this view, but it received a considerable boost in 1913 when the United States first allowed tax deductions for donations made to qualifying nonprofit corporations. This helped cement the perception that activities with high social or spiritual value—education, health care and humanitarian work—are not compatible with a profit motive. By implication evangelism and missions are the least compatible of all. Profit-making activities such as microenterprise development and microbanking are seen as acceptable only because those who profit are the poorest of the world's poor and those who administer the programs are nonprofit organizations. If a large foreign company, especially one with the "multinational" label, promised the same socioeconomic results, it would be viewed by many as opportunistic, or even immoral.

The third reason business and missions are seldom combined is that it creates complications for a ministry's tax exemption. There are, to be sure, significant constraints in place to prevent people from abusing the tax codes. Nevertheless, secular nonprofits now routinely devote substantial portions of their resources to business activities. Those businesses serve many purposes, ranging from merely being a source of income to being an *integral part* of the ministry itself. For example, the YMCA is probably as well known today for its fitness centers as for its ministry to young disadvantaged men. The nonprofit Homeboy Industries is essentially a business set up *by* and *for* former gang members. In the case of the YMCA the fitness center income is likely to be considered unrelated to the organization's purpose and taxable at the normal corporate tax rate. The business of Homeboy Industries, however, is a central part of the organization's rehabilitative purpose, and the income is therefore tax exempt. Hospitals have gift shops, rehabilitation ministries have thrift stores, and universities partner with corporations to share the costs and the revenues of scientific research. Missions organizations are some of the last holdouts. The key legal questions are (1) is the tax-exempt organization legitimately serving a charitable purpose, and (2) is the income from the business related to that tax-exempt purpose? Related or unrelated, there is a great deal of flexibility in how businesses and ministries can work together.

Obviously anyone thinking of bringing nonprofit and for-profit activities together should get competent legal and tax advise first. The point is, businesses—whether working independently or in partnership with nonprofits—can open up many new possibilities for income and ministry. Those who uncritically treat the nonprofit approach as "the way it has always been done" are wrong and are depriving themselves of a powerful tool for ministry. This explains why many forward-looking missions experts are starting to advocate business as one of the most strategic career choices a missions-minded Christian can make in the twenty-first century.

OPPORTUNITIES AND CHALLENGES

The limitless number of ways a business can participate in missions makes it difficult to find a simple way to categorize Great Commission Companies. Some are largely facilitative in nature, created for the express purpose of assisting the work of other, more traditional missions organizations. Others are "pioneers" in the sense that the owners and managers are directly involved in the outreach for which it was created. Some companies are based in highly developed economies like the United States, and others are located in the toughest and most unreached parts of the world. What all the companies have in common is a highly specific purpose and a highly intentional way they go about achieving that purpose. The key is the company's focus and purpose, not its location. The best strategy (business as well as missions) and location depends on many factors, such as the type of business, the economic and religious climate in the country of interest, the status of the indigenous church in that country and so on.

An example of a pioneering GCC, one that is essentially an independent, self-supporting Christian witness, is the Silk Road Handicraft Company, a multimillion-dollar company in Central Asia that employs some three hundred people between its two factories (see chapter seven). About 90 percent of those employees are now Christians, but the most exciting part of the story is the impact these employees are having outside of the factory. They have caught the vision for their own community, and the expatriate management team serves mainly in the background, helping disciple and coach local church leaders. Then there is Seattle-based Bergman Labs, which is doing similar work among unreached peoples living within that city. The founders of this software development company are not only deeply involved in their own church-planting efforts but also help train people for marketplace-based outreach in other countries.

India-based Olive Technology is an example of a "facilitative" GCC, created for the purpose of providing financial and technical support for indigenous Christian ministries in India. The line between a pioneering and a facilitative company is not always black and white, however, and many companies are shades of both. For example, Homestead Partners (see chapter eight) was created for the purpose of providing financial, technological and administrative support for Christian missionaries, but over time this facilitative ministry has led to deep involvement in pioneering work, including investing in pioneering GCCs.

Sometimes the goal of ministering to the neediest and least reached is achieved best by physically locating the company in the country of interest. Other times the goal is achieved more effectively by locating the company in a well-developed and prosperous country like the United States. For example, Seattle-based Pura Vida Coffee was created for the specific purpose of improving the lives of at-risk children in the slums of San José, Costa Rica (see chapter nine). In the process of fulfilling this mission, this seller of fresh-roasted specialty coffee—which is committed by its charter to donating 100 percent of its profit to this cause—raises awareness of the plight of coffee growers in Latin America and helps coordinate the donation of financial and human resources, including short-term missions trips by interested churches and students. The company also gets ministry and marketing "leverage" through fundraising alliances with churches and other ministries such as World Vision, Sojourners and Habitat for Humanity. This is only one example of the seemingly limitless creativity business people can bring to the missionary task of the church.

A company like Pura Vida would almost certainly struggle and fail if located in a less-developed country. However, other companies are facing exactly the opposite problem. The combination of demand- and supply-side pressures is making some companies' very survival dependent on locating some of their production, research and marketing capabilities in other countries. Take Uplift, for example. This Christian-owned maker of motorcycle equipment was being squeezed out of the American market because of high costs and was unable to make any inroads into the lucrative Asian markets for the same reason. It eventually became obvious that the company's survival depended on starting a second production facility in a country like China. The owners recognized this as an opportunity to not only improve efficiencies and break into new markets but also to bless some of the poorest people in the world (see Mt 25:31-40).

SPY, TERRORIST OR MISSIONARY?

One model that has little to commend it is the "missionary in disguise" approach. This is one that uses a business merely as a "cover" for people who quite frankly have little interest in business except for its usefulness as an entry strategy into countries that are off-limits to traditional missionaries. The aim is to do the least amount of work necessary to appear legitimate (at least in their own eyes; few others are fooled so easily). While there have been some churches established this way, the results have been generally mixed, and many Christians now recognize that this "ends justifying the means" approach to ministry is dishonest and a poor witness. The recent exposé on undercover missionaries in *Time* magazine illustrates just how poorly this reflects on Christians as a whole.[10] (To the extent that the article in *Time* has prompted a healthy reexamination among Christians of their methods and motives, it has actually benefited the missions movement in the long run.)

Treating business as a cover and as a distraction from ministry makes as much sense as doctors viewing their work as a distraction from ministry. Furthermore, it often becomes a self-fulfilling prophecy by creating different kinds of pressures. A business that makes no obvious contributions to the local community will quickly raise the suspicions of people who are hostile to Christian missionaries, and there is little preventing such companies from being expelled from the country. This is unfortunate because many of these same countries are quite willing to tolerate legitimate Christian-managed businesses. We have found that the most effective GCCs are in fact quite open about their faith and even have a reputation for evangelistic work. What keeps them from being persecuted or expelled? The value added. Without exception the most secure business "platform" is the profitable, job-creating, tax-paying company.

Why would people feel that they need to fake their way into a country? The answer goes back to the days of colonialism. Despite its faults, one clear advantage of colonialism was the unrestrained access it gave missionaries to less-Christianized countries. Today, without the backing of a colonial power, missionaries are finding it all but impossible to get into those countries. In particular, those countries and nationalities that have a history of being ruled by outsiders are now fiercely protective of their political and economic independence and deeply suspicious of outsiders. While these countries are aggressively trying to attract entrepreneurship and capital from abroad, they have little tolerance for people who make no obvious contribution. Hence the temptation for missionaries to apply for business visas and pretend to be something they are not.

Using business as a cover is neither original nor terribly clever. Missionaries are not the only ones, after all, who use "creative access strategies." Oddly enough, spies and terrorists also have trouble operating openly in most countries, and they too have discovered the usefulness of the business platform. Businesses are routinely used as fronts for all sorts of covert activities. Examples of these undercover operations are rarely discussed publicly, for obvious reasons, but the occasional glimpses we get can help us appreciate the host country's concerns when a business appears to be merely a cover for other, possibly more sinister, activities. For example:

- Long before Osama bin Laden became a household name, his terrorist network used businesses to disguise and fund its operations. For example, the investigation into the 1998 bombing of the American embassy in

Nairobi, Kenya, revealed that at least three business entities—one non-profit and two for-profit firms—were created by bin Laden's network to provide members of his group the legal documents, platform and income necessary to operate freely in that country.[11]

- During the aftermath of President Clinton's pardon of fugitive financier Mark Rich, it was revealed that Rich won favor with the Israeli government in part by allowing his businesses to be used by its intelligence agency Mossad to shield their activities in potentially hostile countries.[12]

- A terrorist group opposed to Iran's current government was recently uncovered in the United States. Through a sham charity called the Committee for Human Rights, this group raised more than one million dollars in donations, mainly at U.S. airports. The money was sent to bank accounts in Turkey, then transferred to an auto parts business in the United Arab Emirates where it was used to buy arms.[13]

People who appear to have hidden agendas are naturally hard to trust. Complicating matters is the fact that the jargon of evangelical missions is now generously seasoned with threatening-sounding metaphors like "targeting" a people group, "establishing a beachhead" and other terms that are easily misunderstood, especially in countries with a history of instability and oppression. September 11, 2001, was a stark reminder that some people believe they are quite literally at war against Christians (and Jews). In an effort to be clear about the humanitarian and transformational purpose of GCCs, we have chosen to refrain from using such terms in this book. By doing so we are following the lead of a cross section of evangelical mission and church leaders and theologians who have pledged to be more careful about their language choices.[14] Without question, there is a very real battle taking place between God and Satan, but we must never create the impression that *people* are the enemy (see Eph 6:12).

THE PURPOSE OF A GREAT COMMISSION COMPANY

What do we mean by "the humanitarian and transformational purpose of GCCs"? Simply put, the good news of the gospel is that in this fallen and pain-filled world, *good overcomes evil*. This Old Testament promise was fulfilled in

Jesus Christ, who then instructed his followers to spread the message that sin and death have been defeated and through Christ we too can have freedom and life (see Jn 10:10). Furthermore, this freedom and life are offered freely to all who believe that Jesus is the Son of God (see Rom 4:25—5:1; Eph 2:8-9; 1 Jn 5:1-5). Many have heard and rejected this message. Many others have never heard the message even once, nor do they see any evidence that good has conquered evil. That is the purpose of a GCC: to bring good news in word and deed to the neediest parts of the world. The good news about globalization is that the barriers that once prevented them from hearing this message are falling and the missions baton is being handed to a new breed of messenger.

Could this be what globalization is about? The success of the apostle Paul's model suggests that Christianity spreads fastest when Christians are not just proclaiming, but also *modeling* the gospel. Could globalization be God's way of bringing business people—perhaps the largest and most underutilized segment of the church—back into missions? What better way to demonstrate and proclaim the love of Christ to a hurting world than through a GCC?

QUESTIONS FOR REVIEW

1. The spiritual-vocational hierarchy is more evident in some churches than in others. What difference do you think such a theological frame of reference makes in the life of a church?

2. Do you know of any "missionaries in disguise"? What has been their experience? What are some of the problems, if any, with this approach?

3. What is the difference, if any, between a GCC and a "missionary in disguise?"

4. What are the key differences a local person would notice, or at least should notice, between a business owned by a Christian and one owned by a terrorist or spy?

5. Visit the website <www.globalopps.org/materials.htm> and read Ruth Siemens's article "Why Did Paul Make Tents?" What are her main points? Go through and find the scriptural references that she alludes to but does not put into the paper. Do you agree with her argument that an authentic tentmaker must be fully self-supported? Why or why not?

2

TOWARD A DEFINITION OF
A GREAT COMMISSION COMPANY

*God calls into being instruments for his purpose to meet the exigencies
of the age and situation.*

DWIGHT BAKER

*The business community—because of its enormous power base of
influence, resources and expertise—is in a unique position to
undertake mission for Christ: worldwide and next door. . . .
The heart of mission is helping hurting people holistically through
the love of Christ. And what matters is not who does it, but who
receives it; not who does it, but how and why it is done.
In these instances, it is the business community itself that is replacing
the traditional "sending agencies" of earlier Christian mission
paradigms. It is the business community utilizing the resources God
has placed in their hands to become a major part of the missio Dei.*

C. NEAL JOHNSON

The term "Great Commission Company" needs to be carefully unpacked.
It is obviously a reference to Matthew 28:18-20, the biblical mandate to
"make disciples of all the nations," commonly referred to as the Great Commission. But what exactly does it mean for a *company* to fulfill this mandate?
Define it too broadly and the term becomes meaningless. Any company doing any good deed at all, no matter how indirectly or unintentionally, would

be included. Define it too narrowly and many Christian-owned businesses would be excluded; or worse, we could be putting all Christians who are working in religiously hostile countries into harm's way. Thus any attempt to define a Great Commission Company (GCC) must begin by addressing the broader questions about the meaning and modern-day relevance of this passage of Scripture and its application to a business context. In this chapter we explain our own theological orientation, introduce some key concepts, then define a GCC.

WHAT IS MISSION(S)?

A subtle shift has been taking place in the terminology used to describe the activity and purpose of the church. To understand the importance of this shift and its relevance to this book, we begin by recognizing that when God created the heavens and the earth, the relationships between God, mankind and creation conformed perfectly to his divine intention and purpose.[1] However, when Satan rebelled against God's authority and established his own competing kingdom, it set into motion a cosmic conflict that will continue until Christ's triumphant return. Therefore sin, properly understood, involves more than a moral failure or a broken relationship with God; it is Satan at war with God, attacking the divine order that was established at creation.[2] Nothing has escaped Satan's corruptive influence. Not only have our relationships with God, each other and nature suffered, but even creation itself has been distorted and damaged (see Gen 3:16-19). As Bryant Myers of World Vision observes, Satan's damage "proved very broad—very holistic, if you will."[3] Accordingly, God's redemptive plan is also holistic, extending not just to individuals but also to the whole of society, its institutions and even to creation itself (see Rom 8:19-23; Eph 1:22-23; Col 1:19-20).

The term *mission* (or *missio Dei*) refers to this singular, all-encompassing plan of reconciliation. In his seminal book *Transforming Mission: Paradigm Shifts in Theology of Mission*, missiologist David Bosch said that Christian mission "gives expression to the dynamic relationship between God and the world."[4] Notice this is a dynamic relationship. It is a living, ongoing story with many chapters. The story of mission begins with the chosen people of Israel and eventually moves to the church through the life, death and resurrection of Jesus Christ. Mission begins with reconciling "us to himself through Christ," who then gives us "the ministry of reconciliation" (2 Cor 5:18). This ministry of reconciliation is, quite simply, the purpose of the church. Indeed, if the church ever ceases to bear witness to God's activity in the world and fails to communicate in word and deed the reconciling message of Jesus Christ, "it has not just failed in one of its tasks," says missiologist Andrew Kirk, "it has ceased being church."[5]

The specific activities of the church (*missio Ecclesiae*) have traditionally been referred to either as "missions" (plural) or "ministry," depending on whether geographical, linguistic or cultural barriers are crossed. Outreach efforts among people of similar language and culture are usually referred to as "ministry," and the term *missionary* has traditionally been applied to those doing crosscultural ministry, that is, "missions." In today's diverse and integrated society, such distinctions can be confusing and even divisive if they appear to reinforce a spiritual-vocational hierarchy. Thus the recent trend has been to eliminate the distinctions and adopt the singular term *mission* exclusively because, after all, almost everything the church does can be seen as part of *missio Dei*. Similarly, it is becoming increasingly common to hear it said that all Christians are missionaries—whether they realize it or not—because whether they are scrubbing floors, selling stocks or teaching Sunday school, they are all instruments of *missio Dei*.

We have chosen to continue using distinct terms for several reasons. First, central to *missio Dei* is the universal glorification of God and the restoration of all creation to a right relationship in harmony with him. In other words, there is a crucial link between physical restoration and spiritual redemption, a link that is often downplayed or overlooked in some of the things that are offered as examples of mission. For example, some comments about "business as mission" or "marketplace mission" make no connection between making widgets and making disciples. To be sure, we can worship God through our work, and there is something about the very nature of entrepreneurship and work that pleases God. But by themselves these things will not necessarily point people to the Savior. Devout followers of other religions also can be creative, honest and hard working, and we cannot assume that people will draw the correct conclusions from our actions alone. At some point the reason for the hope that is within us has to be *verbalized* (see 1 Pet 3:15). Similarly, being a good corporate citizen will not necessarily draw attention to Christ. By definition, missions or ministry involves an intentional effort to make Christ known.

Second, *missio Dei* is perfect and unchanging. However, our human attempts to participate in that plan are imperfect and continually adapting to new social and ecclesiastical conditions. Sometimes these so-called paradigm shifts in missions occur abruptly, such as when Peter recognized in Acts 10 that Christ's sacrifice on the cross was valid for Gentiles as well as for Jews. Suddenly the early church had a new understanding—a new theology, if you will—of God's plan for the church. More often, however, the change occurs gradually, such as when Christianity became the official religion of the Roman Empire in the fourth century and there was, at least in the church as a whole, a subtle shift away from individual conversion and toward the conversion of nation-states. "Evangelism was no longer a personal matter," notes one scholar, "but a matter of joining an institution and following its rituals."[6] Of course, every paradigm has its exceptions. The monks, for example, were the exception to the nominal Christianity of the Middle Ages. Nevertheless, by looking at the sometimes quite remarkable mistakes the church has made over the years, we can see the dangers of equating missions (our collective human response) with mission (God's perfect plan).

The third reason we prefer the distinctive terms is because different kinds of ministry bring different challenges. As missionary statesman Ralph Winter observes, "reaching out in the same culture is relatively simple and is often automatic, while breaking through to a new and different culture is both rare and complex."[7] The apostle Paul's experiences are prime illustrations of this. Much of his early ministry experience was in a similar cultural context. The further away he moved from his cultural roots, the more foreign his gospel became to his listeners, and the more difficult the work became. The point here is not to create a new spiritual hierarchy but to be clear that missions presents a different set of challenges and requires a different kind of preparation than near-neighbor ministry. If everyone is a missionary, the term quickly loses its practical usefulness.

A THUMBNAIL SKETCH OF
PREVIOUS MISSIONS PARADIGMS

The integration of business and missions is seen by many people as representing a paradigm shift in the theology and practice of missions. Put another way, one definition of "the traditional approach to missions" is giving way to another. Some people are uneasy about such talk, suggesting as it does that the old paradigm was flawed. But the truth is, the concept of a "traditional" approach to missions has always been a moving target. No sooner does one approach become traditional and institutionalized then the world changes and the approach is no longer suitable. For example, the full-time, donor-supported missionary—the central figure in the modern missions enterprise—was in many respects an entirely rational response to the combination of colonialism and the Industrial Revolution. Specifically, the dramatic increase in disposable income that began with the Industrial Revolution, combined with the infrastructure of colonialism, made it possible to create a professional class of missionary that could focus exclusively on evangelizing remote parts of the world. One downside, of course, was the impression this eventually created that only some are called into full-time ministry.

Yet before anyone celebrates the emergence of a new paradigm, we must remind ourselves that flaws are easier to spot in the past than in the future. One thing we can say with confidence is that a new paradigm will not be perfect. Below is a sketch to illustrate some of the previous paradigms in missions history.

THE EARLY CHURCH PERIOD (A.D. 30-312). The earliest followers of Christ "began where Jesus told them to begin," observes one scholar, "by loving one another."[i] Moreover, he continues, they followed Christ's example by expressing their love in deeds, not words. "It is a striking fact," notes another mission scholar, "that almost all the proclamations of the gospel which are described in Acts are *in response to questions* asked by those outside the [faith]" (emphasis added).[ii]

A THUMBNAIL SKETCH
(Continued)

Historians have found that, while professional missionaries and pastors did exist during this period, those who were chiefly responsible for the spread of Christianity were regular folks, "men and women who earned their livelihood in some purely secular manner and spoke of their faith to those whom they met in this natural fashion."[iii]

THE MIDDLE AGES (312-1517). After Constantine declared Christianity to be the official religion of the Roman Empire, the church gradually adopted a trickle-down approach to missions whereby the emphasis was on converting the nobility who would then "convert" the entire province by decree. In some extreme cases, missions took a militaristic quality as the outright conquering of peoples became an acceptable strategy for extending the reach of Christianity. By and large, missions was not part of the normal life of individual Christians. Monks did what little evangelism and discipleship took place at the individual level, so those who were the most serious about their faith withdrew from normal life and pursued the contemplative life in a monastery instead.

THE PROTESTANT REFORMATION (1517-1792). One of those ardent Christian monks was Martin Luther, the initiator of the Protestant Reformation. Yet while Protestantism made Christianity accessible once again to common people, Luther believed that the command to preach the gospel to all nations applied only to the original apostles. Furthermore, the Protestant doctrines of predestination and salvation by grace, not works, seemed to provide little theological basis for missions. As John Calvin himself once said, "We are taught that the kingdom of Christ is neither to be advanced nor maintained by the industry of men, but this is the work of God alone."[iv] There was little theological basis during this period for what we would now call missions. There were exceptions, of course, but they tended to be minor and short-lived in nature, and were not representative of the mainstream view.

A THUMBNAIL SKETCH
(Continued)

THE MODERN ERA OF MISSIONS (1792-1970). Given the historical and theological context, it is hard to overstate the importance of William Carey's book published in 1792 titled *An Enquiry into the Obligation of Christians to Use Means for the Conversion of the Heathen.* In the book, Carey argued that the Great Commission was not yet fulfilled and that it was every Christian's responsibility to bring the gospel to those who had not heard. Carey led by example, dedicating the rest of his life to bringing the gospel to India. Others quickly followed suit, and the modern era of Protestant missions was born.

Historian Kenneth Latourette describes the next one hundred years as "the Great Century" in Christian missions.[v] The unity and resolve began to unravel slightly in the early twentieth century, however, when a sharp dispute emerged over the relative importance of social concern and evangelism. Yet, regardless of where a church or denomination stood on this issue, the key players continued to be donation-supported missionaries who would dedicate long periods of their life to "ministry," as they defined it, mostly among the poor and less evangelized.

A NEW ERA OF MISSIONS (1970 TO PRESENT). Some remarkable changes occurred during the last half of the twentieth century—so remarkable in fact that some began calling it a "new world." For example, the end of colonialism and the Cold War opened the door for globalization and postmodernism. Christianity's center of gravity began shifting away from Europe and North America toward Latin America, Africa and Asia.[vi] It would be naïve to think that such fundamental changes did not have an equally profound impact on the church's understanding of what missions and missionaries should look like. One change has been a return to a more holistic understanding of missions, as evidenced by the seriousness given to this subject by both the liberal-leaning World Council of Churches and the evangelical-leaning Lausanne Committee for World Evangelization.[vii] Other changes include a

A THUMBNAIL SKETCH
(Continued)

desire, particularly by younger generations, to integrate work and ministry, to make shorter commitments overseas, and to find ways to avoid the sometimes lengthy process of raising donor support. What some have been calling "less traditional" approaches to missions are gradually becoming more of the norm. Is one approach right and one approach wrong? We think Evvy Campbell of Wheaton College sums it up best when she says that "each generation needs to work through the concepts in its own language and for its own context, looking afresh at biblical and theological foundations, clarifying what properly constitutes holistic mission. . . . This is as true for professional practitioners as it is for laity engaged in mission."[viii]

[i] J. Herbert Kane, *A Concise History of the Christian World Mission: A Panoramic View of Missions from Pentecost to the Present* (Grand Rapids: Baker, 1982), p. 25.

[ii] Lesslie Newbigin, *The Gospel in a Pluralist Society* (Grand Rapids: Eerdmans, 1989), p. 116.

[iii] Kenneth Latourette, *A History of the Expansion of Christianity* (Grand Rapids: Zondervan, 1974), 1:116.

[iv] Quoted in J. Herbert Kane, *A Concise History of the Christian World Mission: A Panoramic View of Missions from Pentecost to the Present* (Grand Rapids: Baker, 1982), p. 74.

[v] Kenneth Latourette, *A History of the Expansion of Christianity* 4 (Grand Rapids: Zondervan, 1974).

[vi] See Philip Jenkins, *The Next Christendom: The Coming of Global Christianity* (New York: Oxford University Press, 2002).

[vii] For discussions of these attempts to move to the center, see John Stott, "Seeking Theological Agreement," *Transformation* 1, no.1 (1984): 21-22; and C. Rene Padilla "Evangelism and Social Responsibility: From Wheaton '66 to Wheaton '83," *Transformation* 2, no. 3 (1985): 27-33.

[viii] Evvy Hay Campbell, "Holistic Mission: Perspectives, Models, and Issues," unpublished manuscript (Wheaton College, 2002), p. 4.

Finally, calling all Christians "missionaries" is problematic in countries where the term carries a great deal of historical and cultural baggage. Many atrocities have been done in the name of missions or with the blessing of missionaries. Rather than foisting a label on Christians that most are not comfortable with, we suggest finding other labels, such as "world Christian" or "kingdom professional," that are more appropriate. In this book we adopt the latter.

WHICH COMES FIRST, THE GREAT COMMANDMENT OR THE GREAT COMMISSION?

Two of the most widely recognized sayings of Christ are the so-called Great Commandment (Mt 22:36-40) and the Great Commission (Mt 28:18-20). Specifically, followers of Jesus Christ should (1) love God with all their heart, soul and mind, and love their neighbors as themselves, and (2) "go and make disciples of all the nations, baptizing them . . . and teaching them to obey" everything Jesus commanded the disciples. Throughout most of church history, these have been understood as two sides of the same coin. That is, our expression of Christ's love through good deeds will prompt others to inquire of us and submit themselves to his benevolent lordship.

However, in the early twentieth century a sharp disagreement erupted between the so-called modernist and fundamentalist Christians over the matter of priorities. (Over time the labels became "liberal" and "evangelical," which we will adopt here.) Is the church's first priority to bring people into a saving relationship with Christ, or is it a more comprehensive (and less specific) ministry of love and reconciliation? The liberals drew heavily from passages like Matthew 22:36-40; 25:31-46; and Luke 4:18-19 and tended to emphasize social action, such as eliminating poverty and promoting human rights. According to the liberal view, as long as we are making the world a better place we are fulfilling God's purpose for the church. The numerical expansion of Christianity, if advocated at all, was a secondary goal, a byproduct of the church's calling rather than its central purpose. Evangelicals, responding to what they saw as an overemphasis on social problems, leaned sharply in the other direction. Drawing from passages such as Matthew 24:14; 8:18-20; Mark 16:15; and Acts 1:8, they focused almost exclusively on evangelism and the saving of people's souls. The numerical expansion of

Christianity was the only objective that mattered, and social work was at best a means to achieving that goal.

In their extremes, both the liberal and evangelical views suffer from very similar flaws. As philosopher and author Dallas Willard points out, they are both "dare we say it—nothing less than a standing invitation to *omit* God from the course of our daily existence."[8] The liberals focus on structural rather than individual sin and, in the process, downgrade the importance of a personal relationship with Jesus Christ. Meanwhile, by relegating God to only spiritual matters, evangelicals have little to say about the earthly relevance of our relationship with Christ. The world, says Bryant, "is left, seemingly, to the devil."[9]

By the end of the twentieth century the evidence was pretty clear: social transformation will almost certainly fail to materialize if either side is neglected. The disappointments are so common, in fact, that in the early 1970s both sides began to return to a more "holistic" understanding of the purpose of the church. Even the World Bank has entered the picture by starting a dialogue with leaders of the world religions about how to integrate physical and spiritual development.[10]

These shifts are certainly encouraging, but the concept of holistic missions is still sufficiently ambiguous as to make it possible to fit almost anything into that label. In practice, old bents and biases usually remain, albeit further below the surface. Thus for the sake of clarity we begin by stating our own assumptions about holistic Christian missions as plainly as possible.

Assumption 1: We have been created for good works. "For we are God's workmanship, created in Christ Jesus to do good works, which God prepared in advance for us to do" (Eph 2:10). Our salvation is not based on works, but good works are *central* to our life's purpose. We are told in Titus 2:14 that we have been purified by Christ to be a people *zealous for good deeds.*

Assumption 2: Good works will create opportunities to share good news. For some Christians, sharing the gospel will be the incidental and serendipitous byproduct of their good works. For others, creating witnessing opportunities is deliberate and intentional. But in either case the outward expression of one's faith will lead to opportunities to "give the reason for the hope that you have" (1 Pet 3:15).

Assumption 3: Authentic missions meets real physical needs, but never stops there. Making a person healthier or more prosperous in this life will never compensate for eternal separation from God. A truly holistic mission strategy addresses *both* the physical and the spiritual needs of a person. If people are not clearly, verbally instructed as to the way of salvation in Christ, we are, in the words of the Lausanne Committee for World Evangelization, "guilty of an inexcusable lack of human compassion."[11] If a community of local believers (that is, a church) does not already exist, there is an effort made to see self-sustaining, reproducing churches spring up in that community.

Assumption 4: Authentic missions aims to draw people into the family of God, but never stops there. The second half of the Great Commission—"teaching them to obey everything I have commanded"—is sometimes overlooked by evangelicals. Missions involves not only preaching, baptizing and planting churches but also creating communities of disciples that are, in the words of Bryant Myers, "full of life and love, *working for the good of the community* in which God has placed it."[12] We would add, "and *beyond* their community."

Authentic missions seamlessly integrates spiritual and physical ministry. It is a cyclical process involving the public display of the freedom and life that is available through Christ (see Jn 10:10), which is attractive, contagious and ultimately leads to new disciples and new churches that themselves meet needs and point others to Christ. Some refer to this cyclical process as "church multiplication" or as a "church-planting movement."

KINGDOM PROFESSIONALS AND MISSIONARIES

Christ expected every one of his followers to obey his Great Commandment and Great Commission. Yet we all know that some Christians are more intentional about reflecting Christ in their everyday life than others. By "intentional" we mean they pray for, prepare for and look for opportunities to meet needs and tell people about Jesus. These are not obnoxious, in-your-face evangelists but people who take seriously the apostle Peter's instruction (1) to *be ready* to tell others and (2) to do it with "gentleness and respect" (1 Pet 3:15). Both readiness and presentation can be improved with preparation and experience. Intentional Christians simply take preparation and experience more seriously than others. Those who are the most consistently effective also allow themselves to be held accountable to their outreach goals and spiritual growth.

There are different levels of intentionality. In fact it can be viewed more as a continuum like the one in figure 2.1. The distinction between intentional and less-intentional Christians is not black and white. But, as Gary Ginter of Intent correctly points out, "at some point along that progression, the difference in degree becomes so large that it is more correctly seen as a difference in kind."[13] For simplicity we will distinguish between two types of intentional Christians. First, there are professional Christian workers who assist in the spread of Christianity as part of their *vocation*. It is what they are gifted, trained and *paid* to do. Those who are paid to do this crossculturally are "missionaries." Second are what Ginter calls "kingdom professionals," those who are called and gifted for service in the marketplace. They are equally committed to Christ and to showing their faith, but they earn their living in some other way. They see their profession not as a distraction from ministry but rather as the *necessary context* through which relationships can be built and Christ can be revealed. Kingdom professionals recognize the intrinsic value of work; that work itself is an integral part of God's holistic, redemptive plan for the world. But they take their calling a step further, seeking to make the most of their God-given opportunities to impact the people around them and measuring success according to their contribution to what God is doing.[14]

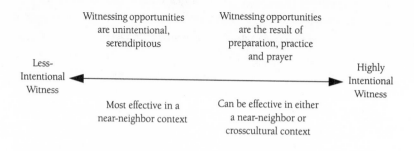

Figure 2.1. Continuum of intentionality

By making these distinctions it is not our desire to introduce a new spiritual hierarchy but rather to point out the obvious fact that some Christians give more thought to ministry and missions than others. Those who are not as intentional can, and quite often do, have a meaningful, positive impact in people's lives. But their efforts are guided more by happenstance than by planning, prayer and accountability. Moreover, because of their uneven experience and training, their impact is usually limited to people of similar language and culture (also known as near-neighbor outreach). As cultural and linguistic distance increases, so does the likelihood of misunderstandings and miscommunications. Put another way, the more similar in background two people are, the easier it is to (1) recognize when the other person is hurting or is curious about our faith and (2) convey our concern for their welfare "with gentleness and respect." By comparison, effective crosscultural outreach generally requires more time, experience and training. Simply put, it requires more intentionality in training and effort.

The archetypical model of a kingdom professional is the apostle Paul. It is safe to say that his only desire in life was to preach the gospel (see 1 Cor 9:16) and see churches spring up in the spiritually driest places (see Rom 15:20). That was his motive—his passion, if you will. His *strategy*, however, was unconventional, at least by today's standards. From all indications in Scripture, Paul worked a great deal (see Acts 18:1-3; 20:34-35; 1 Cor 4:11-13; 1 Thess 2:9; 2 Thess 3:8). He apparently did not think of his work as a distraction from ministry; otherwise he would have dropped it without a second thought. After all, he gave the strongest defense in the Bible for supporting missionaries and pastors (1 Cor 9). So why did he work? A careful study of his letters reveals that working was a central part of his missionary strategy. Spreading the gospel for free added credibility to his message and served as a model for his converts to follow (see 1 Cor 9:12-18). Demonstrating that missions is the responsibility of all Christians was arguably the single most brilliant part of his mission strategy and the reason why his churches spread so rapidly.[15]

Missionaries and others in "full-time ministry" almost by definition have trouble fitting into the warp and woof of society. Take for example Jeff Nolan, founder of the Silk Road Handicraft Company (see chapter seven). Before moving to Farstan, Jeff was in a full-time discipleship ministry that involved meeting men for breakfast, studying the Bible with them, praying with them and so on. After breakfast the other men would go to work and he would go home. Today Jeff no longer considers that authentic discipleship ministry because he had no shared life with those people. It was a teaching ministry but not discipleship. Not until he started working *alongside* people in Farstan did he discover what true discipling is all about. "We now have lots of time together and they get to see me 'do it,'" Jeff says. "When I mess up, I model the other part too and say, 'This is what a Christian does when he messes up.'"

Missiologist Andrew Kirk says that missions is about getting people to "stop, look and listen."[16] Since many people take an interest in the message of Jesus Christ only after seeing the gospel in action, this means that the *messenger*, as well as the *message*, is important.[17] Paul seems to have understood this. Priscilla and Aquila also must have understood this. These tentmaking professionals were deeply involved in church planting ministries in at least three different cities—Ephesus (Acts 18:19), Rome (Rom 16:3-5) and Corinth (1 Cor 16:19).

Could one of the problems with our missionary efforts today be that we send so few lay Christians into less-evangelized contexts and expect so little out of those we send?

CAN A BUSINESS BE AN INTENTIONAL WITNESS FOR CHRIST?

Like the distinction between intentional and less-intentional Christians, there is a continuum of *corporate* intentionality as well (see figure 2.2). At one end is the "Christian company." Obviously companies cannot be "saved" in any meaningful sense, but to the degree that they reflect biblical values and behave "Christianly" in other ways, this can be a useful term. Christian companies typically are known for treating their employees, customers and suppliers with dignity and respect, and they have a reputation for integrity and high ethical standards. Many go a step further by supporting community activities and by placing Scripture verses and other inspirational messages in prominent places, such as in their corporate lobbies, on their packaging materials and in their public relations literature. Like the Christian individual, Christian companies can and quite often do have a positive impact in their communities. But the process is usually more serendipitous than intentional. It is not centrally coordinated or the result of planning, equipping or accountability. By comparison, GCCs are characterized by a higher level of intentionality and accountability.

Company has a reputation for integrity, fairness and consistently high-quality work.

Missio Dei drives the mission and vision statements and core values.

Witness is almost exclusively in the form of deeds, not words.

Ministry plan calls for visible and verbal witness that results in new communities of faith through facilitation and pioneer efforts

Christian Company ← → Great Commission Company

Company founded primarily with near-neighbor witness in mind.

Company founded primarily for the purpose of seeing Christ revealed to least-evangelized peoples.

Figure 2.2. A continuum of corporate intentionality

The distinction can be brought into sharper focus by asking the following questions: Are drawing people into the family of God and promoting their spiritual growth central parts of the organization's purpose? Is there a well-understood link, besides tithing out of wages and dividends, between the business plan and the ministry goals? Is the upper-level management held accountable to those goals? Clearly most Christian companies do not fit this definition of a GCC. Indeed some leaders in the Christian business community would argue this is an entirely inappropriate function of business. But is it? For example, one pillar in the Christian business community recently told a journalist for *Fortune* magazine, "We can't and shouldn't and don't want to drive people to a particular religious belief." Instead, he said, the company wants people to "ask the fundamental questions. What's driving them? What is this life all about?"[18] These obviously are important questions that we should be encouraging people to ask. But who will be there to provide answers? A Scientologist? A Muslim? Does it matter? Are there people within the company who take an active role in prompting these questions? Is there a system in place for making sure those who are asking these questions are getting the proper attention? Is upper-level management held accountable for the spiritual impact of the company? Perhaps these are unreasonable expectations to place on large, publicly owned companies like the one profiled in the *Fortune* article. But while some companies may be constrained legally and culturally, there is no reason why other firms cannot be more intentional and proactive in their approach.

THE CHARACTERISTICS OF A GREAT COMMISSION COMPANY

There is no limit to the forms a GCC can take. Nevertheless there are some basic characteristics that they all have in common, which enable us to define a GCC as

> a socially responsible, income-producing business managed by kingdom professionals and created for the specific purpose of glorifying God and promoting the growth and multiplication of local churches in the least-evangelized and least-developed parts of the world.

A GCC is socially responsible. It unapologetically strives to earn a profit, which is a clear indication that real needs are being met and resources are being used wisely. But the company does not seek profit at any price. GCCs are equally concerned about the wages, the working conditions and the professional development of their workers (see Prov 21:13; 22:16). GCCs do not exploit the environment or lax government oversight for short-term gain. When appropriate they even help with such things as education and health care for workers' children (see Gal 6:10).

A GCC is an income-producing business. These are authentic businesses that create value-added products or services. Unlike the nonprofit model that is sustained by the zero-sum transfers of wealth from one person or group to another, GCCs *create* wealth. Their ability to sustain themselves means that money is not siphoned away from other ministries. Indeed,

GCCs often help sustain other ministries as well.

A GCC is managed by kingdom professionals. Kingdom professionals strive for excellence in their work. They view their gifts as a strong indication of God's intended role for them in the body of Christ.[19] Their work often becomes the springboard for discussions about matters of faith. The most qualified will have some training and experience in crosscultural outreach. While there may be some nonbelievers at the management level of the company, it is essential that those in key decision-making positions be kingdom professionals if the company is going to reflect Christ. Ideally the team will comprise a range of spiritual gifts and be multinational and multigenerational.

A GCC brings glory to God. A GCC draws attention not to itself, but to the Lord and Ruler of the company—Jesus Christ (see Mt 6:33). It is important to remember that these companies focus on bringing the good news to places that are the most challenging in economic and spiritual terms. Without exception the spiritual resistance will be significant. This means that the most effective GCCs are those managed by people well grounded in the spiritual disciplines. When the pressure is on, they do not drift into the secular or generally accepted ways of doing things. God is then glorified when suppliers are paid in a timely manner, customers are treated honestly and with respect, the poor receive appropriate attention, and the rich are not cheated. In many cases such behavior runs counter to the cultural status quo. Such contradictions to culture help bring clarity to Christianity and eventual confession of Jesus Christ.

A GCC promotes the growth and multiplication of local churches. The larger community almost immediately notices a GCC's atypical behavior. This enables GCCs to participate either directly or indirectly in the growth and multiplication of local churches. Formal alliances are often formed with indigenous churches and ministries in the area. The focus is always on building up the *indigenous* church rather than on trying to transplant the nonessentials that are held dear in our own cultures.

A GCC's main focus is on the least-evangelized and least-developed parts of the world. Without devaluing the work being done among already-evangelized people, the GCC's main goal, like the apostle Paul's, is to bring the gospel where Christ is not known (see Rom 15:20). Of course, as we have said before, this may include pockets of people in our own neighborhoods and cities. Or it may include equipping others for crosscultural marketplace ministry, as Bergman Labs in Seattle and Soil Solutions in Maryland are doing. Nevertheless the principal focus is on the less-evangelized and less-developed countries.

MINISTRY MODELS

There is no limit to the creativity that can be unleashed when people start thinking outside the nonprofit box. However, the limitless variations make it difficult to come up with a simple way to classify the different approaches. For simplicity we have chosen to isolate two variables. First is the company's level of independence. As we will see, some companies work very closely with missions organizations, even going so far as to have a contractual relationship. We call these *alliances*. An example would be Global Engineering and Management Solutions, a company that works in close partnership with more than a dozen agencies (see chapter ten). Every kingdom professional working for the company has an accountability relationship with a church or agency and a contract that outlines the responsibilities and expectations of each party. Similarly, Pura Vida Coffee is bound by a contract at the organizational level, one that keeps it accountable to the ministry in Costa Rica for which it was created (see chapter nine). The Silk Road Handicraft Company (see chapter seven) and Homestead Partners (see chapter eight) are comparatively more independent in nature. Their goal is to assist the work of other churches and agencies, but they are not legally accountable to those groups in any formal way.

The second variable is the nature of the company's participation in the missions effort. A *facilitative* GCC, such as Homestead Partners, sees its role largely as providing logistical support for those on the field. Likewise Pura Vida helps support the ministry in Costa Rica. On the other hand, a *pioneering* GCC is more directly involved in the actual ministry activities. Like the continuums developed earlier in the chapter, these categories are not black and white, and the distinctions between GCCs are more often like distinctions between shades of gray. While the difference between, say, the Silk

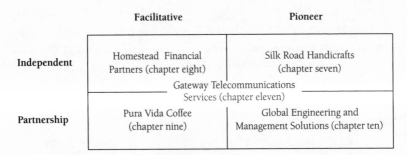

Figure 2.3. Typology of Great Commission Companies

Road Handicraft Company and Pura Vida Coffee is fairly clear, the separation between Homestead Partners and Pura Vida Coffee is much smaller. Then there are companies like Gateway Telecommunications Services that defy easy classification because they are a blend of all four categories.

The purpose of this typology is simply to provide a starting point from which we can illustrate some of the different facets of GCCs. No value judgments should be made based on this model, since they are merely different types of GCCs.

QUESTIONS FOR REVIEW

1. It was noted that if the term "Great Commission Company" is defined too broadly it becomes meaningless and if defined too narrowly it would exclude most Christian companies. What is an example of a broad definition? A narrow definition? How would you define a GCC?

2. Dallas Willard has said that both the liberal and evangelical interpretations of Christian discipleship are "nothing less than a standing invitation to *omit* God from the course of our daily existence." How can God be omitted under a liberal interpretation? Under an evangelical interpretation? Do you agree with Willard? Why or why not?

3. Visit the website of the Evangelical Missiological Society and read David Hesselgrave's article "Holistic Christianity? Yes! Holistic Mission? No! . . . and Yes!" (<www.missiology.org/EMS/bulletins/hesselgrave.htm>).

In this article, Hesselgrave argues against the idea of holistic mission, saying that Christians ought to be holistic, but strictly speaking, Christian mission is "exclusive and specific and, . . . only in a secondary sense is it holistic." Do you agree? Why or why not?

4. What is meant by the term *intentionality?* Give some examples of how individual Christians can behave intentionally. Do you agree that an intentionality continuum like the one in figure 2.1 exists? How can a business be intentional about advancing the gospel?

5. What is meant by the term *accountability?* How can individual Christians be held accountable? How might you go about holding a company accountable to ministry goals?

6. What do you think the businessman meant when he said, "We can't and shouldn't and don't want to drive people to a particular religious belief. [We want them to] ask the fundamental questions. What's driving them? What is this life all about?" What is your opinion of this statement?

3
GLOBALIZATION AND BUSINESS

*The great paradox of [globalization] is that its new technologies
enable people and nations to take sudden leaps into modernity, while
at the same time they promote the renewal of once-forbidden
barbarisms. Amid the newness of things, exploitation of the weak by
the strong also flourishes again.*

WILLIAM GREIDER

*Global free trade is a Faustian bargain. A nation sells its soul for
a cornucopia of foreign goods. First the nation gives up its
independence; then its sovereignty, and finally its birthright—
nationhood itself.*

PATRICK J. BUCHANAN

*The raw fact is that every successful example of economic
development this past century—every case of a poor nation that
worked its way up to a more or less decent, or at least dramatically
better, standard of living—has taken place via globalization; that is,
by producing for the world market rather than trying for self-
sufficiency. Many of the workers who do that production for the global
market are very badly paid by First World standards. But to claim that
they have been impoverished by globalization, . . . you have to forget
that those workers were even poorer before the new exporting jobs
became available and ignore the fact that those who do not have
access to global markets are far worse off than those who do.*

PAUL KRUGMAN

A central part of our thesis is that globalization is a part of God's plan to integrate the entire body of Christ into his global plan (mission). In particular, those who have been taking more of a spectator role over the last century are suddenly being thrust into the game, to use Ed Silvoso's analogy. Our focus has been on business professionals, but the reemergence of laypeople in missions is much more widespread and is being driven by the declining barriers—economic, political and social—that once kept people apart. The cumulative effect of these crumbling barriers has been a dramatic increase in the exchange of products, services, information and culture, and a corresponding increase in crosscultural human interaction. While some suspect a new phase of colonialism by the West,[1] there is considerable evidence of a two-way flow of influence. For example, a growing share of multinational business activity originates *in* the developing world. Our neighborhoods, schools and workplaces are becoming more multinational and multiethnic every year.

Yet as we can see from the quotes at the beginning of this chapter, the question of whether or not globalization is improving the quality of life on planet Earth is highly controversial, and the debate often gets very emotional. As is so often the case when intelligent people disagree, there is an abundance of evidence that can be used to support either position. For example, in the last ten years alone the percentage of people living in poverty worldwide has fallen from 29.6 to 23.2 percent.[2] This translates into almost *four hundred million* people who, while still desperately poor, no longer face the daily threat of starvation. Since 1950 the average consumer's purchasing power has nearly tripled worldwide, as measured by real (inflation-adjusted) per capita gross domestic product.[3] Put another way, the average young person today can afford nearly three times the goods and services that

Region	GDP per capita 2001 (current dollars)	Average Annual Growth (percent)		
		1971-1980	1981-1990	1991-2000
World	5,260	1.8	1.3	1.2
High-income economies				
United States	36,332	2.2	2.2	2.2
Japan	32,858	3.3	3.5	1.1
European area	20,114	2.7	2.1	1.7
Asian newly industrialized economies*	16,195	7.2	5.9	4.7
Low- and middle-income economies				
Asia	737	3.0	4.8	5.4
East Asia and Pacific	956	4.6	5.6	6.4
China	912	4.3	7.7	9.0
South Asia	468	0.7	3.4	3.3
Latin America and Caribbean	3,678	3.3	−0.9	1.6
Eastern Europe and Central Asia	2,101	2.5	0.7	−1.9
Middle East and North Africa	2,099	3.6	−0.6	1.0
Sub-Saharan Africa	454	0.5	−1.2	−0.4

*Includes Hong Kong, Singapore, South Korea and Taiwan.

Figure 3.1. Growth of real per capita GDP, by region. Source: World Bank (*Global Economic Prospects 2003*).

his or her grandparents were able to buy when they were the same age. (Any grandparent will be happy to verify this.) Substantial progress also has been made in other areas of human development, such as a 42-percent reduction in the infant mortality rate since 1970, an eight-year increase in the average life span, a 50-percent increase in the adult literacy rate and a five-fold increase in the percentage of rural families with access to safe water.[4]

Another undeniable fact about globalization is that many people are being left behind. As figure 3.1 shows, per capita gross domestic product (GDP) varies widely, and the gap between rich and poor countries is the widest ever recorded. This reflects the fact that while most countries are growing, some are growing at a far slower pace than others and in some cases even moving in the reverse direction. As figure 3.1 also shows, GDP growth has been relatively stagnant in the Middle East and North Africa for the last twenty years and has been declining in sub-Saharan Africa and the former Communist countries. Furthermore, while it is true that the *percentage* of people living in poverty has fallen sharply, the absolute *number* of poor people has remained almost unchanged due to the relatively faster population growth in the poorest countries. Many of these same countries have also experienced reversals in life expectancy, child mortality and other measures of development.

With such starkly contrasting ways to interpret the data, it is not surprising that agreement about what should be done has been illusive. One thing almost everyone agrees on, however, is that there is no single problem or solution. Every country is a product of a unique set of political, cultural, historical and geographical circumstances that inhibit its ability to adapt to a rapidly changing world. For example, United Nations sanctions, civil wars and lawlessness have disabled the economies of many countries. Local customs and geographic isolation have hindered progress for some others. Many of the problems in sub-Saharan Africa—declining life expectancy, for example—can be attributed to the AIDS crisis that is sweeping across that continent. And finally, policymakers in industrialized countries and the interest groups that influence them bear some responsibility for the unhappy circumstances in the developing world.

Blaming globalization for these problems, however, is like blaming rain for a leaky roof. Rain *exposes* a problem with the roof and can sometimes make an existing problem worse, but strictly speaking, the rain is not the problem. Contrary to what many well-intended protestors may think, reversing the trend toward economic integration is likely to hurt more people than it helps. The truth is, no one benefits from a contracting economy, and most countries *want* to be plugged into the global economy but some find themselves for various reasons on the sidelines. The appropriate question Christians and other concerned citizens should be asking is not "How can we stop the rain?" but rather "How can we help protect and repair some roofs?"

The church is uniquely qualified to assist in this area because of its multicultural, global constituency and its biblical mandate to put others first. It is therefore entirely appropriate for Christians to enter this debate, to assist in enterprise development, to teach, live and do business in these countries, and to seek ways to create the socioeconomic conditions necessary for economies to prosper. Yet before the church can credibly participate in this debate, it must become better informed about how economies grow and how globalization can benefit the world's poorest people. On this score, Pope John Paul II deserves a great deal of credit for the obvious effort he has made to understand the issues from all sides.[5] The following quote is one of many public statements he has made on the subject that reflects the thoughtful and nonreactionary way he is approaching this issue.

> The processes that are globalizing markets and communications do not in themselves possess an ethically negative connotation, and therefore a summary and *a priori* condemnation of them is not justified. . . . Globalization will have many positive effects if it can be sustained by a strong sense of the absoluteness and dignity of all human persons and the principle that earthly goods are meant for everyone.[6]

The more typical response by Christians and Westerners in general tends to be rooted in a self-centered obsession with the impact (real and perceived) globalization is having on *our* lives and *our* interests, rather than on how we can use our resources more effectively to promote the economic and spiritual development of countries that are suffering. The purpose of this chapter is to bring some clarity to this often misunderstood subject by providing a broad overview of the causes and consequences of globalization, with an emphasis on the role of foreign direct investment and the implications for GCCs.

THE CAUSES OF GLOBALIZATION

Globalization is a widely used term because it affects almost every area of modern life. In economics the term refers to a few key developments in the area of international economic activity. One of those developments is the increasing relative importance of international trade. For example, in 1950 only 8 percent of the world's total output crossed national borders; by 1998 this figure had increased to 26 percent.[7] This means that an increasing share of what one country produces is being bought in other countries, and vice versa, which implies that our economies are becoming more interdependent.

Another indication of this growing interdependence is the dramatic increase in foreign direct investment (FDI). The United Nations Conference on Trade and Development (UNCTAD), which tracks international production and foreign investment, estimates that there are over 65,000 multinational corporations with ownership linkages to some 850,000 foreign affiliates worldwide, a figure that has more than *tripled* between 1995 and 2001.[8] In addition, there are "an (unknown) number of firms . . . that are linked to each other through non-equity relationships."[9] In terms of dollar value, FDI outflows have increased over 1,200 percent between 1982 and 2001, far outpacing the 170 percent growth of international trade during the same period.[10] Already the idea of a product's or corporation's "nationality" seems almost quaint, argues one international business expert.

Is IBM Japan an American or a Japanese company? Its workforce of twenty thousand is Japanese, but its equity holders are American. Even so, during the 1980s, IBM Japan provided, on average, three times more tax revenue to the Japanese government than has Fujitsu. What is its nationality? . . . Are they "American" products? If so, what about the cellular phones sold in Tokyo that contain components made in the United States by American workers who are employed by the U.S. division of a Japanese company? Sony has facilities in Dotham, Alabama, from which it sends audiotapes and videotapes to Europe. What is the nationality of these products or of the operation that makes them?[11]

Finally, dwarfing either of these trends is the stunning increase in the cross-border flow of international currencies. Between 1973 and 1995, for example, foreign-exchange turnover increased from $15 billion to $1.2 trillion *per day*.[12] As we have seen in recent years, the ability to easily move billions of dollars from one country into another has a frightening potential to bankrupt countries almost overnight.

Behind these trends are two powerful forces: technology and economic liberalization. Examples of the former include rapid advances in the communications and information technology industries that have made it possible for even the smallest firms to do business in other countries. The ability to share data and remain in close contact with people a continent away also means that many services that were once considered nonexportable, such as health care, education and computer programming, have become international industries. Similarly, innovations in the transportation and refrigeration industries have expanded the range of goods that can be sold internationally. Harvard economist Jeffrey Frankel observes that "now fresh-cut flowers, perishable broccoli and strawberries, live lobsters, and even ice cream are sent between continents."[13]

The most dramatic illustration of economic liberalization was the abandonment of socialism by the Soviet Union, followed by the more controlled transition to a free-market economy by China. Probably more significant, however, have been the eight rounds of completed trade negotiations under the General Agreement on Tariffs and Trade (GATT). When GATT was created in 1947, only twenty-three countries participated in the initial negotiations to reduce trade barriers. Today some 145 countries are participating in the ninth round of talks (the Doha Round). Largely because of these negotiations, the average tariff levels of industrialized countries on imported manufactured goods have fallen from an average of 40 percent in the 1940s to less than 4 percent at the conclusion of the Uruguay Round (1987-1993).

The growing number of countries participating in GATT negotiations reflects the abandonment by many developing countries of their post-colonialism experiments with protectionist, inward-oriented approaches to economic development. In theory, excluding foreign competition can stimulate development by giving domestic firms the breathing space necessary to grow and become efficient enough to compete on a global scale. In practice these policies failed because the firms were not only shielded from competition but also from the incentives to innovate and improve efficiency. These policies led not only to lower-quality products but also to a lower quality of life that became increasingly difficult to defend politically. As a result, all but the most tightly controlled governments are now easing their restrictions on imports as well as foreign investment. Almost every government now recognizes that "in a liberalizing and globalizing world, growth can be sustained only if countries foster new, higher value-added activities, to produce goods and services that hold their own in open markets."[14]

There are many dimensions to the process of fostering "new, higher value-added activities." For starters, it requires upgrading a nation's workforce, capital base and infrastructure—monumental tasks, especially for developing countries. The process can be accelerated by "importing" capital from abroad through foreign aid, foreign borrowing or foreign direct investment and, in particular, by attracting world-class companies that have access to global networks of technology, managerial talent and other resources that are on the cutting edge of the "new economy." Not surprisingly, almost all countries are now aggressively seeking to attract foreign companies and making the necessary regulatory changes. According to UNCTAD, an overwhelming 93 percent of the regulatory changes made worldwide between 1991 and 2001 were aimed at making national economies more attractive to foreign companies.[15]

However, there are other dimensions to economic development that are only indirectly related to a country's physical resources. These have to do with the overall business environment. How widespread is the corruption problem? Are property rights and other contracts enforced? Do the citizens have a sense of belonging to society? That is, do they feel it is within their power to help improve their society? The more dysfunctional a society is in these areas, the more difficulty it will have attracting resources from abroad.

THE SIMPLE ECONOMICS OF INTERNATIONAL TRADE

Imagine if Nebraska—a state rich in fertile soil, clean water and natural resources—decided to close itself off from the rest of the United States economy in the interest of protecting itself from outside competition and stimulating its economy. Achieving this goal would require the state to become self-sufficient by shifting resources—land, labor and capital—out of crop and livestock production and into the production of clothing, furniture, lumber, tools, cars, gasoline, rubber, toys, building materials, school supplies and so on. The reallocation of resources and production would be great news for the employees of these newly "expanding" industries but very bad news for those who earn their living in the state's agriculture and livestock industries. It would also be bad news for those who enjoy such things as coffee, tea, seafood, most fruits, Caribbean vacations and other things that simply cannot be produced in Nebraska. The adjustment process would be slow and painful, and the net effect would be a sharp reduction in the value of the state's total output because its resources would no longer be employed in the most productive way.

Nebraska specializes in producing crops and livestock because, quite frankly, no one can produce crops and livestock as well with a given quantity of land, labor and capital. Nebraska is certainly capable of producing other things, but it gets the most bang for its resource buck by specializing in these industries, which is the beauty of free trade: it helps an economy identify the most valuable use of its resources. By lowering its barriers to trade and investment, a country gradually begins to use its existing resources more productively, specializing in the industries that are most suited to its resources. Both imports and exports increase, but because production in its strongest industries increases and production in its less efficient, disadvantaged industries decreases, the net effect is an increase in the value of the country's total output.

Many countries have tried unsuccessfully to improve their economic competitiveness by restricting the flow of foreign goods and resources

THE SIMPLE ECONOMICS OF INTERNATIONAL TRADE (Continued)

into the country. While such protection benefits certain well-organized interest groups within the economy, these policies harm the country as a whole because the firms are shielded not only from competition but also from any incentive to innovate and improve efficiency. History has shown that these policies ultimately lead to lower-quality products and a lower standard of living. Most countries that once thought this was the way to catch up have abandoned their experiments with protectionist approaches to economic development and are now easing their restrictions on imports and foreign investment.

Some may argue that the Nebraska analogy is a weak one because in the United States trade occurs between states that are relatively equal in terms of wages, education levels, labor and environmental standards, and so on. Yet a closer look reveals significant differences even within the states, *which is precisely why trade between the states is beneficial*. North Carolina gains by importing cheap orange juice from Florida and using its own resources to create higher-value products like furniture instead. Likewise, it is cheaper for Floridians to import furniture than to produce it themselves. But even if we accept that the states are similar in many ways, this is clearly a *consequence* of the freedom to move goods and resources between the states, not a precondition for such beneficial trade. Likewise the poorest economies will grow faster and experience a more rapid improvement in their quality of life if they are able to use their resources in the most productive way. This in turn requires that wealthy countries allow the fruits of their labor into their countries. Yes, they will be more cheaply priced than our domestically produced goods, and some will call this "unfair" or the result of an uneven playing field. But from the developing countries' perspective, those goods represent the most valuable use of their resources. Rather than trying to prevent those imports using fallacious and self-serving arguments, Christians should be doing everything they can to encourage trade with less-developed countries.

Thomas Friedman, author of *The Lexus and the Olive Tree,* correctly points out that "there is now a growing awareness among leaders of developing countries that what they need in order to succeed in the globalization system is not just an emerging market but . . . an emerging *society*" (emphasis added).[16]

This then is the basic dilemma for developing countries: they recognize that it is in their best interest to strive for *social* as well as *economic* transformation. Yet sustainable social and economic change requires more than mere changes in policy. It requires transformation of the minds and hearts of the very citizens who have seen little reason to trust the government or to hope for a better future. It requires shedding one worldview that rationalizes cheating, corruption and cronyism and replacing it with one that encourages transparency, honesty and respect for authority. As the experience of the former Soviet Union has shown, capitalism without an internally consistent and generally accepted set of values will fail just as surely as any of its alternatives. The transformation of individuals as well as institutions is so vital to the development process that organizations such as the World Bank and US-AID have even started supporting research and other efforts aimed at strengthening the moral and social foundations of these economies.

The implications for the Christian business professional are obvious. Social, economic and spiritual transformation is, in the words of missiologist Andrew Kirk, "quite simply, though profoundly, what the Christian community has been sent to do."[17] Businesses, like individuals, can be agents of transformation, for good or for evil. For every example of a reckless or exploitive company, there are at least as many examples of companies that are making a positive difference in these countries. Even if the stereotype about multinational corporations is true, that merely strengthens our case for GCCs because the ministry impact will be even *greater* as the contrast between Christian and non-Christian companies becomes clearer.

WHY ARE BUSINESSES GOING GLOBAL?

Ironically, one of the consequences of global economic integration is a progressive *disintegration* of the production process. By disintegration we mean that large, vertically integrated firms that produce everything themselves are giving way to global networks of smaller, more flexible and entrepreneurial firms that are linked together by a variety of equity and non-equity relationships. Such networks enable firms to share resources, risks and rewards while maintaining a degree of independence and flexibility.

It is commonly believed that the main reason firms locate parts of their operations in foreign countries is to avoid the high wages and strict regulations of their home countries. This of course presupposes that wages and regulations are the main things that influence a firm's location choice. The evidence, however, does not support such an assumption. If true, then the global flows of FDI would be mainly one-directional—that is, flowing *out* of high-wage, highly regulated countries and flowing *into* those that have lower wages and less government regulation. While this is true for some industries, the majority of the evidence indicates an overwhelming preference for locating in industrialized and more regulated countries. Western Europe alone typically attracts more foreign capital than all developing countries combined, and the highly regulated U.S. economy attracts almost *nine times* more FDI, on average, than its poorer and less-regulated neighbor, Mexico.[18] The truth is, only about a third of all FDI flows into low-wage, less-regulated countries, in spite of their aggressive efforts to lure more foreign capital.

Even more problematic for those who believe firms are motivated only by regulations and wages is the increasing share of FDI flowing in the *opposite direction*. Specifically, the share of the total FDI outflows originating from developing countries nearly doubled between 1987 and 1998, from 7 to 13.9 percent.[19] Firms headquartered in Asia have been the most active in this area, although UNCTAD has also noticed a nontrivial increase in foreign investment by firms headquartered in Eastern Europe and Latin America.

A wage-centric theory of foreign investment simply cannot explain why a growing number of firms headquartered in developing countries are locating some of their assets in the high-wage, highly regulated countries within North America and Western Europe. This is not to say that wages and regulations are unimportant. But a more complete and nuanced explanation for why firms are "going global" must take into account the substantial pressures on the demand side of the industry. Economic liberalization means that firms are facing more competition and more informed and sophisticated consumers than ever before. Firms can no longer expect to build market share and profitability by staying at home but must continually look for new markets. They must provide service that is faster and better, and products that are more specialized to the needs of local consumers. Only by looking at the demand side can one explain why firms are locating not just production but also marketing and even research and development capabilities in or near every market in which they hope to do business.

For those who adapt well to this new environment the rewards can be substantial. But so are the risks. Managing employees from an unfamiliar culture and maintaining acceptable levels of quality and productivity are just a couple of the challenges that have bedeviled even the largest multinationals. As one pair of experts recently noted in a top management journal: "Despite the attractiveness of these newly opened markets, stories of business failures resulting from lack of understanding of local firms abound; increased interactions with indigenous firms in these countries are frequently accompanied by frustration and failures."[20]

Furthermore, as many as 40 percent of Western business professionals who are given foreign assignments return early, and many of those who stay suffer from a range of problems including depression, marital problems and alcoholism.[21] The point here is that, were it not for the pressures on the demand side of the market, few firms would take the plunge. But globalization is making "playing it safe" a less viable option and is indeed *forcing* companies of every kind and size to invest in foreign countries—a convenient fact considering that many of those same countries are now off-limits to missionaries.

DOING WELL BY DOING GOOD

From a developing country's perspective foreign firms bring resources and skills that are in short supply, although the degree to which a country actually benefits from those resources depends as much on local economic factors as it does on the firm itself. For example, the extent to which a foreign firm's know-how and technology can "spill over" and benefit the local economy depends on the skill level and technical capabilities of the local firms. As the capabilities gap between foreign firms and domestic suppliers increases, the likelihood of such "backward linkages," the key to beneficial spillovers, decreases. Similarly, if domestic firms do not enjoy the same business-friendly treatment that foreign firms receive—tax incentives, lower tariffs and so on—it can put them at a competitive disadvantage and undermine the chances for beneficial backward linkages between foreign and local firms.[22] Naturally there is only so much a single firm can do about problems of this nature. Nevertheless, there are other things a firm *can* control, or at least look for, that will enhance the development potential of its investment. We have grouped these into four main categories—capital, employment, technology and know-how, and foreign exchange—and conclude with an application to GCCs.

Capital. One of the most obvious and immediate benefits of FDI to a host economy is the inflow of capital. When capital is scarce, an economy cannot maintain, much less expand, its productive capacity. A country importing foreign capital is similar in some respects to a firm that borrows money to expand or upgrade its capabilities. One disadvantage of foreign capital, however, is that it has the potential to leave the country as quickly as it came, which can cause serious economic disruptions. Of all the possible ways to import foreign capital, FDI is particularly attractive because businesses tend to stay put longer than other investors and come with fewer strings and conditions. Furthermore, larger multinational corporations have the potential to undertake large-scale projects that are especially conducive to economic development. In response to the risk of "capital flight," many developing countries also impose restrictions that are designed to discourage pulling capital (or profits) out of the country too quickly.

Employment. FDI can also create new jobs, although the net effect depends on several factors. First, it depends on whether a new company is created (also known as a "greenfield" investment) or an existing company is acquired. Naturally, fewer new jobs are created in the latter case. Jobs can also be indirectly created as a result of the expanded activities of local suppliers and indirectly lost if the larger and more efficient foreign firm drives local firms out of business. The latter tends to be more of a problem when foreign firms enter for the purpose of introducing their own brand of products to the local markets, which has the potential to drive out the indigenous brands.

Technology and know-how. Probably more important than either the capital or the jobs are the proprietary assets a firm brings, those things that cannot be easily copied or reproduced, such as world-class technologies, specialized skills and established networks of managerial and marketing know-how. Companies that have been isolated from foreign competition typically lag decades behind in these areas and are therefore unable to compete effectively in world markets. Foreign firms help remedy this when they link up with local firms for materials and components. In the interest of securing reliable, high-quality materials, foreign firms often provide technical assistance, training and other services to help bring the local suppliers up to an acceptable level of competence and efficiency.[23] The experience gained in this way also enables local firms to compete more effectively at home and abroad.

Foreign exchange. FDI can also help shore up a country's supply of foreign exchange, although this too depends on several factors. First, the initial inflow of capital represents an injection of foreign currency, although this must be weighed against the extent to which the firm relies on foreign sources for its materials and components. (The typical pattern is for multinational corporations to rely heavily on imports in the early stages but to gradually import less as local firms become more reliable and efficient.) The second factor is the firm's purpose. Does the firm sell its output in foreign markets (and thus bring in currency) or in domestic markets? Many countries offer special incentives to encourage firms to import less and/or export more.

IMPLICATIONS FOR GCCs

While the implications for GCCs may seem obvious for some, they are far from simple. If a GCC ignores basic economic principles it puts both the business and its ministry impact at risk. For example, it might be tempting to say that "a GCC should never lay off workers" or "a GCC should always use local sources," but a company that fails because of an oversized payroll or because it tolerated inferior materials does no one any good in the long run. Ultimately these are decisions that must be made on a case-by-case basis. The best we can do is point out how a company can be the most beneficial, recognize that every situation is different, and leave it for the GCC management to choose the most appropriate actions.

- ***Do no harm.*** GCCs should exemplify the best qualities of a socially responsible corporation and seek to minimize the direct and indirect costs of its business to the host country.

- ***Choose the right industry.*** Think twice about setting up a business that introduces consumer goods to the local market, particularly those that are already being produced by local firms. Instead use the company as a base for exports.

- ***Help the local economy modernize.*** There is little benefit from entering a country and doing what local entrepreneurs can already do. Bring businesses that will *upgrade* the technologies and skills available locally. Link up with local suppliers as quickly as possible, and take steps to raise their level of competence and efficiency.

- ***Be an incubator.*** Take steps to promote creativity and entrepreneurship within the company as well as in the supplying firms. Plan on doing at least some research and development locally. Whenever feasible, create spinoff companies and/or satellite offices that are managed by nationals.

- ***Be a local philanthropist.*** Plow some profits back into the local economy. Be as generous as possible with wages. Repatriate profits sparingly. Work with charities and nongovernmental organizations to identify needs and distribute aid.

GCCs are not suitable for every economy and every situation. Some countries simply do not have the infrastructure or resources to support a company that aims to compete on a global scale. In those cases microenterprise development and other strategies are the best answer, at least in the short term. But even then the goal should be to create links as quickly as possible with world-class companies that are competitive in global markets.

QUESTIONS FOR REVIEW

1. Aside from the Great Commission implications, do you think the net effect of globalization is generally good or bad? How so?

2. What role do you think the church has in the globalization debate? Has

the church been an effective participant in that debate?

3. In addition to bringing business to less-developed countries, what are some other changes Christians can make in their behavior that will benefit the world's poor?

4. This chapter discussed the economic impact of FDI. What are some non-economic impacts of foreign investment?

5. In his book *Profits and Principles,* Cornell University professor Michael Santoro maintains that Western companies impart radical new ideas and values that help foster democracy and human rights in these countries. Is this good? What other values (good or bad) might be getting transmitted?

6. Do you believe a GCC should make as many "backward linkages" as possible, even if it compromises the profitability of the company?

7. What can a GCC, perhaps in partnership with other Christians, do to enhance the beneficial spillovers?

4

GLOBALIZATION AND MISSIONS

*And this gospel of the kingdom will be preached in the whole world
as a testimony to all nations, and then the end will come. (Mt 24:14)*

*After this I looked and there before me was a great multitude that no
one could count, from every nation, tribe, people and language,
standing before the throne and in front of the Lamb. They were
wearing white robes and were holding palm branches in their hands.
And they cried out in a loud voice: "Salvation belongs to our God,
who sits on the throne, and to the Lamb." (Rev 7:9-10)*

Christianity enjoys a global reach that is unparalleled in its history. By anyone's count, it ranks as the largest world religion. According to the most recent *World Christian Encyclopedia,* almost one-third of the world's six billion people identify themselves as Christian, that is, "followers of Jesus Christ as Lord, of all kinds, all traditions and confessions, and all degrees of commitment." About 650 million of these are "evangelicals," meaning their faith is centered on a living and personal Jesus, they are committed to the evangel (the gospel) as set forth in the Bible, and they seek to spread the gospel by means of their day-to-day personal witness and their participation in organized Christian ministries.[1] The most remarkable growth has been in places like Cambodia, Bangladesh and Nepal where, largely because of the efforts of national believers who are taking the Great Commission seriously, the number of Christians has been growing exponentially. Similar growth has been taking place throughout Africa and Latin America. In Africa, for example, the Christian population has grown from about ten million in 1900 to a staggering 360 million by 2000, and researchers estimate that Latin America will assume the title of "Most Christian Continent" by 2025 with some 640 million believers.[2]

There is no longer any question, notes Ralph Winter of the U.S. Center for World Mission, that the gospel transcends culture, that it is for all peoples, that it makes sense in any language and that it is "not merely a religion of the Mediterranean or of the West."[3] Yet despite this apparent progress there are many indications that the job is far from complete. Many people are still suffering and oppressed, have not had an opportunity to make an informed decision about Christ's message and are persecuted and ostracized if they respond affirmatively. In this chapter we identify some of the trends and challenges related to missions and discuss their relevance to GCCs.

WORLD MISSION TRENDS AND CHALLENGES

Globalization of all world religions. In his book *The Next Christendom: The Coming Age of Global Christianity,* Philip Jenkins persuasively argues that Christianity is not in decline, but rather its center of gravity is merely shifting from the wealthy northern countries of Western Europe and North America to the relatively poor southern countries in Latin America, Africa and Asia. While he is arguably too generous in his definition of *Christian,* there is no doubt that some of the most exciting things happening in the church today are taking place outside of the "Christian" West. But Christianity is not the only religion going global. Many traditionally non-Western religions have been migrating westward, and followers of those religions can now be found in nearly every major European or American city. According to one student of global religious trends, Hinduism and Buddhism are currently the fastest growing religions in Australia, and Islam is the fastest growing religion in Europe.[4] This means that our neighborhoods, schools and workplaces are becoming more religiously and ethnically diverse. An array of foods, sports, music and religions that were once foreign to us are becoming more familiar. But more importantly, crosscultural outreach that once required traveling to a foreign country can now be done at home in places like the lunchroom or the local park.

Globalization of the mission force. The dramatic growth of the church in non-Western countries is also giving rise to a new generation of missions, one that is being driven increasingly by the churches in those countries. For example, many countries that were once the destination for Western missionaries—such as South Korea, Brazil and Nigeria—are now "net sending" countries, meaning they send more missionaries than they receive. One source estimates that some 95,000 of the estimated 419,000 missionaries sent out in the year 2000 originated from non-Western countries.[5] Estimates such as these are always fodder for good debates, however, because everyone seems to have his or her own criteria for who should and should not be counted. Length of service, whether or not the person is working in a different culture or being supported (financially and otherwise) through a missions agency—these are just a few of the variables that make quantification difficult. But one thing is undeniable: an increasing share of the work is being done by non-Western believers and by people—such as kingdom professionals—who are feeling less constrained by traditional expectations and definitions.

Globalization of partnerships. A growing number of organizations—agencies, churches, academia—are recognizing the importance of teamwork, networks and partnerships. The day of the lone ranger is over. The complexity of the task (recruitment, selection, training, member care and so forth) and the competencies and resources required to be effective are beyond any single organization. Like corporations in the for-profit world, the missions community is discovering the value in creating a niche area of specialization and is partnering with others to create synergy and unity. In many cases, Westerners are coming alongside as partners rather than leaders of local church-planting efforts. They have discovered that one of the secrets behind self-sustaining indigenous church-planting movements is to hand the leadership of the movement over to national believers as quickly as possible. Thus a growing number of these teams, networks and partnerships are being led by national believers rather than Westerners, another indication of the increasing role of non-Westerner believers in global missions.

Challenge of the unreached. It is obvious from these trends that the life-transforming message of the gospel, once understood within the context of a person's own culture and language, will resonate with people from any tribe, tongue or nation. Everywhere the gospel has been planted, people take "ownership" of it and (unless discouraged by an overly paternalistic missionary) take it upon themselves to spread that message to others within their group. Yet until they first *hear* the gospel in a culturally relevant way, they remain unevangelized. The term "unevangelized" should not be confused with "unsaved." There are many people who have heard and understood but rejected (at least for now) the gospel. For statistical purposes they are considered evangelized, albeit still nonbelievers. Some countries, such as the United States, are considered largely evangelized, even though there are clearly many people who refuse to let Jesus be the ruler of their lives. Yet even in a country like the United States, a significant number of people are still unevangelized. Even though they have access to Christian television and radio, the cultural-linguistic gap is so wide in some cases that the listeners simply cannot comprehend the message they are hearing. This explains why it is still vitally important for Christians from all ethnic groups and nationalities to continually make an effort to understand the cultures and worldviews of those around them.

Another distinction is often made between reached and unreached "people groups." A people group is defined as "the largest group within which the gospel can spread . . . without encountering barriers of understanding or acceptance."[6] Here again we have a reference to the cultural and linguistic barriers that can inhibit the gospel's progress. The Joshua Project has identified 16,800 people groups worldwide. Of these, roughly 10,400 have been "reached" in the sense that "there is an indigenous community of believing Christians with adequate numbers and resources to evangelize itself."[7] As seen in figure 4.1, almost all of the unreached people groups are located in the Eastern hemisphere, with the heaviest concentrations in what is sometimes referred to as the 10/40 Window because it approximates the areas bounded by 10 degrees and 40 degrees north of the equator.

We should keep in mind, however, that while the 10/40 Window has helped the church focus on the importance of unreached peoples, there is still much work to be done outside of the window as well. For example, there are pockets in South America that are just as unreached as the Middle

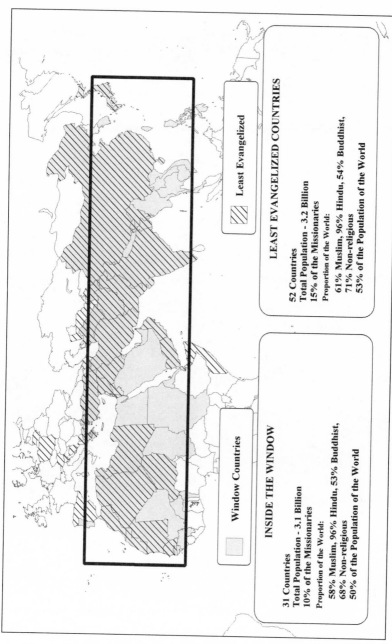

INSIDE THE WINDOW

31 Countries
Total Population - 3.1 Billion
10% of the Missionaries
Proportion of the World:
58% Muslim, 96% Hindu, 53% Buddhist,
68% Non-religious
50% of the Population of the World

Window Countries

LEAST EVANGELIZED COUNTRIES

52 Countries
Total Population - 3.2 Billion
15% of the Missionaries
Proportion of the World:
61% Muslim, 96% Hindu, 54% Buddhist,
71% Non-religious
53% of the Population of the World

Least Evangelized

Figure 4.1. The least evangelized countries and the 10/40 Window. Source: Global Mapping International. Data from Operation World CD-ROM 2001.

Region	Number of people living on less than $1 per day (millions)			Share of population (%)		
	1987	1990	1999	1987	1990	1999
East Asia and Pacific	418	486	279	26.6	30.5	15.6
Excluding China	114	110	57	23.9	24.2	10.6
Eastern Europe and Central Asia	1	6	24	0.2	1.4	5.1
Latin America and the Caribbean	64	48	57	15.3	11.0	11.1
Middle East and North Africa	9	5	6	4.3	2.1	2.2
South Asia	474	506	488	44.9	45	36.6
Sub-Saharan Africa	217	241	315	46.6	47.4	49.0
Total	1,183	1,292	1,169	28.3	29.6	23.2
Excluding China	880	917	945	28.5	28.5	25.0
Region	Number of people living on less than $2 per day (millions)			Share of population (%)		
	1987	1990	1999	1987	1990	1999
East Asia and Pacific	1,052	1,114	897	67.0	69.7	50.1
Excluding China	300	295	269	62.9	64.9	50.2
Eastern Europe and Central Asia	16	31	97	3.6	6.8	20.3
Latin America and the Caribbean	148	121	132	35.5	27.6	26.0
Middle East and North Africa	65	50	68	30.0	21.0	23.3
South Asia	911	1,010	1,128	86.3	89.8	84.8
Sub-Saharan Africa	357	386	480	76.5	76.0	74.7
Total	2,549	2,712	2,802	61.0	62.1	55.6
Excluding China	1,797	1,892	2,173	58.2	58.7	57.5

Figure 4.2. Income poverty by region, selected years. Source: World Bank (*Global Economic Prospects 2001* and *2003*).

East. Some European countries considered "reached" are largely unevangelized because, in spite of their Christian heritage, fewer than 1 percent of the
people have any meaningful understanding of what Christianity is about.

Challenge of poverty. Many of the same countries that are considered unevangelized or unreached, particularly those in the 10/40 Window, are also
suffering from crushing poverty and oppression. As figure 4.2 shows, in 1999
there were almost 1.2 billion people—*almost a quarter of the world's population*—who struggled daily just to survive. The World Bank's definition of poverty—which takes into account only the income necessary to sustain a human
life—currently stands at $395 per year, or $1.08 per day (commonly reported
as one dollar per day). Using a more generous figure of two dollars per day,
nearly half of the world's population, or 2.8 billion people, lives in poverty.

Looking at individual regions, we see that the number of people in poverty
in East Asia fell dramatically between 1987 and 1999. It also fell in Latin
America and the Middle East. The number of poor people in South Asia, however, rose slightly, even though the *percentage* of people in poverty fell (from
about 45 percent to 36.6 percent). In Eastern Europe and Central Asia the
number in poverty soared both in absolute terms (from one million to twenty
four million) and relative terms (from 0.2 percent to 5.1 percent of the population). Likewise, in sub-Saharan Africa both the number and percentage of
poor people increased, with now almost half its population (49 percent) living
on less than one dollar per day. Such abject poverty often leads to frustration,
hopelessness and despair and sows the seeds for local and global terrorism.

According to some observers, even more troubling than poverty itself is the
growing gap in the per capita GDP of rich and poor countries. At the beginning of the twentieth century, per capita GDP in the richest economies was
about nine times higher than in the poorest. By the end of the twentieth century that gap had grown to somewhere between forty-five to one and seventy
to one.[8] The concern here is that if the poorest economies' growth is outpaced
by the rich economies, the result is an inescapable feeling that "the poor are
getting poorer." History has shown that there are few things as socially desta-
bilizing as a sharp increase in income inequality. Today's situation is potentially
even more volatile because advances in communications technologies have
made it easier for the poor to actually see how far they are falling behind. For

this reason a growing number of political and economic experts are beginning to see this as the most urgent global poverty problem.[9]

Challenge of persistent religious persecution. Every study of religious persecution has found that, while no religion is immune to persecution, Christians by and large are the most persecuted of all religious groups. One observer recently noted, "On a worldwide basis, Christians are the most persecuted major religion in terms of direct punishment for practicing religious activities—public worship, evangelism, charity."[10] Many Christians are persecuted to the point of death. In fact, according to one recent estimate there were more Christians martyred during the twentieth century than in all previous centuries combined.[11] Figure 4.3 shows that, with few exceptions, the severest persecution takes place in or near the 10/40 Window. A recent study commissioned by Freedom House's Center for Religious Freedom came to a nearly identical conclusion. Specifically, the study found that the countries with the least religious freedom were located in Asia, North Africa and the former Soviet Union (Central Asia).[12] Organized by religion, their results showed that countries that are predominately Buddhist or Islamic enjoy the fewest religious freedoms.

Challenge of dwindling resources. Another discouraging trend has been the steady decline in resources being sent to the most oppressed and least-reached countries. As we can see in figure 4.4, of the $270 billion donated each year to Christian churches and ministries, only .02 percent, or $54 million, goes to fund the work being done in the least-evangelized countries. Figure 4.5 looks at the distribution of resources in another way: according to the number of missionaries (per million people) working in each major cultural-religious bloc. As we can see, in Muslim countries there are fewer than three missionaries per million, compared to almost 186 per million serving among largely Christianized people groups. The point is, whether we are talking about money or people, the overwhelming majority of our efforts and resources are directed toward the wealthier and already evangelized parts of the world.

APPLICATION TO GREAT COMMISSION COMPANIES

In his highly acclaimed book *The Clash of Civilizations and the Remaking of World Order*, Samuel Huntington makes a convincing argument that the world is entering a new era, one in which religion and culture will replace

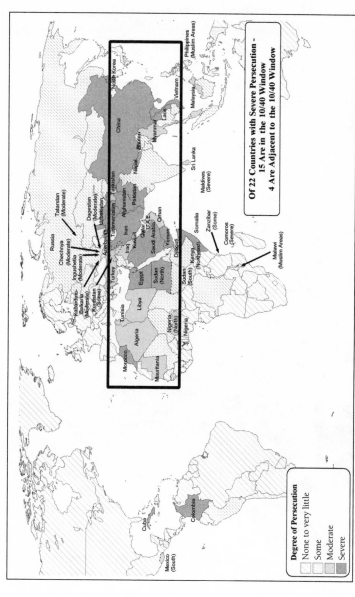

Figure 4.3. Christians under persecution and the 10/40 Window. Eighty-six percent of countries with severe persecution are in or adjacent to the 10/40 Window. Point ranking taken from Open Doors International Persecution List, July 2001, <www.gospelcom.net/od/>. Categories created by Global Mapping International; map by Global Mapping International.

ideology and economics as the main source of geopolitical instability. We are seeing some evidence of this trend, particularly in the Middle East and parts of the former Soviet Union, and some of the issues discussed in this chapter are also consistent with that prediction. However, we would add that many conflicts that appear to be religious or cultural in nature often have economic roots as well. In other words, we believe economics will continue to be an important source of tension, particularly if the gap between rich and poor continues to grow unabated.

Given that Christians earn approximately one-quarter of all the income in the world, we have a choice: we can either be the focal point of much of the envy and bitterness in this world or a source of blessing and hope. One way we can bless the poor is to carefully assess our lifestyle choices and our positions on such things as free trade and foreign investment, particularly the impact these policies have on less-developed countries. Another way to bless the poor is for Christian business owners to be more intentional about leveraging their company's assets and networks for the benefit of the world's poor. Investing in the poorest countries—what some are calling the "bottom

Where money given to the church is going

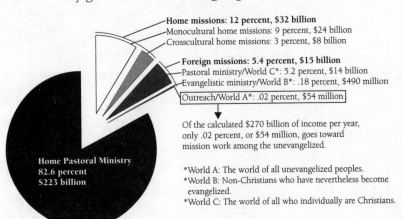

Home missions: 12 percent, $32 billion
Monocultural home missions: 9 percent, $24 billion
Crosscultural home missions: 3 percent, $8 billion

Foreign missions: 5.4 percent, $15 billion
Pastoral ministry/World C*: 5.2 percent, $14 billion
Evangelistic ministry/World B*: .18 percent, $490 million
Outreach/World A*: .02 percent, $54 million

Of the calculated $270 billion of income per year, only .02 percent, or $54 million, goes toward mission work among the unevangelized.

*World A: The world of all unevangelized peoples.
*World B: Non-Christians who have nevertheless become evangelized.
*World C: The world of all who individually are Christians.

Home Pastoral Ministry
82.6 percent
$223 billion

Figures reflect money given by the Church worldwide in U.S. dollars.
Due to rounding, totals may not add up exactly.
Source: World Christian Encyclopedia, 2nd Edition, New York: Oxford University Press, 2001

Figure 4.4. Giving to missions. Source: *Mission Frontiers,* September 2001, p. 11.

of the pyramid"—not only can make good business sense but can also lift countless people out of poverty and remove one of the prime motivations behind social unrest and terrorism.[13] Such transformation, however, will require a change in priorities in the West at the individual, corporate and national levels, and Christians ought to be leading the way.

Then there is the matter of the church's spiritual agenda. While some people may scoff at the idea that religion matters, the truth is that there is now ample evidence showing that some cultures and religions are more conducive to economic progress than others.[14] Christianity in particular holds up quite well when matched up against the socioeconomic impact of other religions. Study after study has shown that remarkable things happen in communities—at both the micro and macro levels—when the gospel is clearly articulated and accepted. For example, in a recent study of evangelical Protestantism in Colombia, Elizabeth Brusco found that conversion led to a sharp reduction in the negative behaviors—excessive drinking, gambling and extramarital affairs—commonly associated with the machismo culture.[15] The change in priorities of the husbands led to equally dramatic

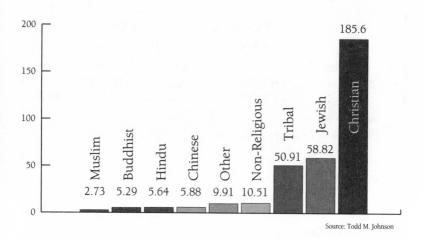

Source: Todd M. Johnson

Figure 4.5. Number of foreign missionaries in major cultural blocs. Source: Todd M. Johnson. This material is extracted from *Perspectives on the World Christian Movement Reader* (Pasadena, Calif.: William Carey Library, 1999) and *Mission Frontiers* (June 2000). Reprinted with permission.

INTERESTING PEOPLE-GROUP FACTS

1. There are approximately 11,200 ethnic people groups identified in the Joshua Project database. There are about 16,800 if each people group is counted once per country of residence.

2. There are about 8,200 people/country groups in the world (out of 16,800) with less than 10,000 individuals, in addition to about 1,200 for which no population has been reported (but the population is probably small). For all those groups, the total number of individuals is less than 20,000,000.

3. The Mandarin Chinese is the largest people group, being in 98 countries with a total of about 793,000,000 individuals, and with 783,000,000 of those in China.

4. India has the largest number of ethnic people groups, 2,329 in the Joshua Project database. (The number of people groups in India varies greatly depending on the researcher and how the term "people" is defined. Strictly linguistically there are about 330-350 "peoples" in India. Some suggest the 2,329 groups in the Joshua Project list should be subdivided into groups by Indian state, producing a total of about 4,700).

5. Papua New Guinea is the runner-up in number of people groups, at 907. Interestingly, the largest group of those 907 is only 270,000 in population. The total population of the country is only 5,200,000, yet there are over 900 people groups. Indonesia (793) and Nigeria (596) follow Papua New Guinea.

6. On the other end of the spectrum, South Korea only has seven people groups, with a country population of 48,400,000.

7. There are over 1,000 languages/dialects spoken in Papua New Guinea. There are only 35 languages/dialects spoken in Japan, which has a population over 25 times as large as Papua New Guinea.

God has made an incredible mosaic of peoples, cultures and languages!*

*Source: <www.joshuaproject.net/peoplefacts.html>

improvements in the standard of living for women and children because money was reallocated for the families' housing and education. Similarly, Amy Sherman found that in Guatemala, conversion from what she calls "Cristo-paganism" to evangelical Protestantism resulted in many of the same socioeconomic improvements.

> The adoption of a morally rigorous protestant ethic . . . frees believers from alcohol addiction and encourages careful, disciplined investments in family well-being. It also encourages families to avoid potentially harmful traditional remedies for illness and saves money previously expended for [these services]. Some converts, it appears, pursue literacy with a new energy. . . . Families are able to save more of their income, which is then often invested in housing improvements and children's education. Moreover, they enjoy stronger family relationships and avoid the expenses often formerly incurred by the husband's fighting, gambling and loss of work time following drinking binges.[16]

In both studies, the transformations at the family level had widespread benefits as entire communities experienced revival. This powerful combination of social and spiritual transformation is precisely what is meant by the "holistic" nature of *missio Dei*. Pursuing either agenda by itself is inconsistent with the purpose of the church.

Within this context, there are seven reasons why Great Commission Companies are uniquely positioned to reach a hurting world.

- While poverty is nothing new, never before have so many people been so aware of what they lack, so open to change and so eager to partner with the business community to help them reach their destination faster.

- A properly motivated world-class business can contribute to economic growth, social progress and spiritual hope.

- Never has it been so easy to travel and communicate internationally but so difficult to go as a professional missionary.

- Global economic pressures are compelling businesses to develop a more global perspective about their markets and supply chain.

- Jobs provide a dignified means to support one's family and for Christians to support the work of their local church.

- More than any time in recent history, Christian laypeople want meaning in their work and are looking for ways to integrate their faith into their work.

- The workplace provides a real-life setting where values, ideas and biblical principles are exchanged, observed and tested.

It is easy to see why many missions-minded Christians are now reconsidering the impact business professionals can have in the twenty-first century.

QUESTIONS FOR REVIEW

1. How well do you think Christianity is doing in fulfilling the Great Commandment and Great Commission? Where are the gaps?

2. Are there any people in your neighborhood, school or workplace that you think fit the definition of unevangelized? What steps can you take to understand their culture well enough to be able to convey the gospel to them in a meaningful way?

3. How would you define *poverty?* What do you think the Bible means when it talks about "the poor"?

4. How would you answer the question, "What's so good about the good news?"

5. How does ministry in a workplace context differ from other contexts?

5

TURNING VISION INTO ACTION

Then I heard the voice of the Lord saying, "Whom shall I send? And who will go for us?" And I said, "Here am I. Send me!" (Is 6:8)

In the first four chapters we looked at how globalization is paving the way for businesses to play a more direct role in fulfilling the purpose of the church. In this chapter we look at the steps necessary to launch a GCC, followed by a discussion in chapter six about governing a GCC. Because every situation is different and presents its own unique challenges, these should be treated as general guidelines rather than hard-and-fast rules. The process also depends on whether we are talking about a well-established business or a startup company. The steps described below are applicable in both cases, although our main focus will be on startups. The startup process begins with some feasibility research, fundraising and recruitment, followed by more fundraising, more research and more recruitment. In other words, it is an iterative process whereby steps are continually revisited and refined. The goal will be to create a business plan and a "Great Commission plan" that provide answers to the questions investors and other stakeholders will ask.

For illustration purposes we will use the hypothetical example of a thirty-year-old chemical engineer named Cedric who has developed a new kind of ink that he believes has the potential to significantly reduce the problem of counterfeiting. Cedric would like to turn this into a GCC but needs to test, market and produce the unpatented product first, something that he estimates will cost one million dollars. Another obstacle is his lack of business experience; he has never started or managed a business. Through various friendships and connections, however, he eventually meets a like-minded fifty-year-old man who has successfully taken several companies through the startup, ramp-up and exit phases. After much discussion and prayer, they agree to combine efforts, contribute fifty thousand dollars each and embark on the adventure of a lifetime—launching a GCC.

We will follow Cedric through the steps in a typical GCC startup process:

- Evaluate the business opportunity.

- Evaluate the missions opportunity.

- Assemble a management team.

- Build an advisory network.

- Develop a business plan.

- Develop a Great Commission plan.

EVALUATE THE BUSINESS OPPORTUNITY

The most promising business ideas are those that address a relatively unmet need. The more urgent the need or the problem, the more valuable the solution will be. On this score Cedric's innovation has the potential to be quite valuable because counterfeiting is a significant and costly problem in many countries. For a business to be successful, however, it must have more than just a good idea. It must have some kind of competitive advantage or "barrier to entry" that makes it difficult for others to copy the idea and compete away the profits. For Cedric this may (or may not) be the patentable technology. For others it may be brand recognition or unique managerial talent or economies of scale that require even new entrants to be very large. Without an obvious way to differentiate your product or service and keep competitors at bay, a business may never get off the ground because the likelihood of recovering its initial startup costs is low. Therefore before pursuing a business opportunity it is important to ask the following questions:

- How large is the market?

- What makes the business unique?

- Is the idea financially viable?

Many other questions must be addressed by the time a business plan can be drafted, but these three questions will be enough for an initial evaluation.

How large is the market? An aspiring entrepreneur must begin by understanding who the customers are, why they need the product or service, and how much they would be willing to pay. Harvard business professor Amar Bhide has found that the most successful entrepreneurs are those who find solutions to problems they encountered in a previous job.[1] One advantage these people have is that they already understand the customers' problem and the potential value of the solution. In contrast, only 20 percent of Bhide's sample came up with the idea "serendipitously" through a relative, a magazine article or, in one case, while on a honeymoon in Italy. In these cases, much more research is required to get a realistic sense of the market siz and the revenues the business can expect.

Those percentages are probably reversed in the case of missionaries seeking to become business owners. Many start by first identifying a country or people group, often after visiting the country once or twice, then proceed to sort through—rather serendipitously—possible business ideas. A common "solution" is to start an import-export company, where the typical pattern is to find a product first—say, beautifully handmade scarves—then look for a market for the product. We could fill several books with the stories of struggling import-export companies that put the cart before the horse in this way. Occasionally a company will succeed, but more often it merely sets people up—customers, suppliers, employees—for disappointment and failure. There is simply no substitute for identifying a customer first, knowing what his or her needs are, then finding competent manufacturers who can reliably meet the customer's specifications.

Cedric would do well to get a better feel for the problem of counterfeiting. Which countries are plagued by this problem, and what is the cost to those countries? At first glance, it would seem that the market potential for Cedric's innovation is huge because counterfeiting is a significant and costly problem in many countries. But before he puts too much effort into developing the product he should gather more information about the nature and scope of the problem.

What makes the business unique? One must also consider the potential competition, both known and possible future competitors. If the idea has any merit at all, competition will be inevitable and profits will likely be short-lived. This can be especially true for markets that are large and relatively undifferentiated, such as Internet service, which raises the possibility of companies being overrun by larger and more efficient competitors. We know of at least one GCC that inadvertently got caught in this situation and had to choose between growing and selling the company quickly or getting squashed by a large multinational. Choosing the latter strategy would force them back to the drawing board, so to speak. Choosing the former strategy would potentially result in a huge payoff that could be used to bankroll other ministry efforts. The management team chose the former. We are not in a position to second-guess that decision. All we know is that as an ongoing presence in an unreached country, the company unfortunately has been overtaken by market forces.

The best markets will be large enough to allow for significant growth but fragmented enough to have defensible niches. Starbucks Coffee probably would never have succeeded had it taken on the whole coffee industry. Instead it successfully exploited a small (but surprisingly not so small) niche: the gourmet coffee market. Likewise the most promising GCCs are those that find niches in which they enjoy certain competitive advantages based on such things as unique managerial talent, brand recognition, efficiency, quality or a hard-to-replicate technology. Without something that clearly distinguishes the company's product or service from others, the company's long-term prospects are not good. Once established in the market, caution must also be taken to avoid complacency. There are few things, including patents, that cannot be bypassed or imitated if given enough time. A company's long-term survival requires a continual process of innovation and improving service.

Cedric's innovation is potentially patentable, but whether that will offer the protection he needs is another question. A better strategy may be to *not* patent the technology and keep it as a closely guarded trade secret instead. At some point in the near future he will need to seek competent advice because the application for a patent is something he will want to start as soon as possible. He should also start thinking ahead about what other competitive advantages his company might have.

Is the idea financially viable? Not until the market has been clearly de-fined and the company's distinctiveness identified can we start talking about the financial viability of a business opportunity. This is not necessarily a function of size. Small businesses that serve small markets—a local coffee shop, for example—can be profitable if the initial investment is low and the product or service is distinctive enough to fend off imitators. As the risks and investment size increase, there needs to be a corresponding increase in the expected return, or investors will look elsewhere for more attractive risk-return opportunities. This is true even when the investor is a kingdom-minded Christian and the investment being considered is a GCC.

The experience of the Strategic Capital Group—a company that helps raise venture capital for GCCs—is an enlightening illustration of this point. They have found that many wealthy Christians would rather donate their money (and receive an immediate tax deduction) than *invest* in a high-risk venture in a less-developed country. Even when there is a significant proba-bility of both a spiritual and a financial return on the investment, investors tend to scrutinize a for-profit opportunity much more rigorously than they will a donation.

That being the case, the management team should be prepared to answer the following questions:

- How much money will it take to turn this into a profitable business?

- Where will the money come from?

- What other resources will be required (management skills, technologies and so on)?

- What is the expected timeline for payback?

- How "mobile" are the assets? If things go badly, can they be redeployed or sold?

- How flexible is the business model? Is there room for expansion, changes in direction or alliances with other companies?

- What will be the return on investment?

Many people who aspire to start a GCC search far and wide for kingdom-minded investors who are willing to accept a low return (in the neighborhood of 5 to 10 percent). Given that some of the safest investment opportunities also earn this much, it is often difficult to persuade people to accept that same rate for a high-risk venture. Some investors can be found at these rates, but generally speaking there is a limit to how much capital can be raised that way. The more serious entrepreneurs should have a clearly identifiable plan for growing the company and for producing a 25- to 50-percent annualized return for the investor. This is not to say that the annual interest rate or dividend needs to be that high, but the investment should be structured so that the total expected return is high enough to compensate for the added complexity and risk.

Cedric's venture will likely require several "rounds" of financing. The first round will be to develop the product (or in some cases, a prototype) and find at least one customer. A minimum of one more round of financing will be required to ramp up the production and marketing efforts. We can see that, in his case, the startup costs are likely to be high and the payback period could be several years, but the risks are offset by a payoff that is potentially quite high.

EVALUATE THE MISSIONS OPPORTUNITY

As with financial value, GCCs that have the most significant *missional* value are those that address a relatively unmet need. There is nothing necessarily wrong with redundancy, that is, outreach efforts that overlap, taking place where others are already working or where the population has already been heavily evangelized. But good stewardship demands that we *consider the most strategic use for our resources.* The most strategic role of a business will depend on the nature of the business, the countries in which it operates and the status of missions in those countries. The following questions will help the entrepreneur identify the key issues.

- What location or people group will benefit the most from this type of company?

- What can this company do that other Christian organizations in the area cannot?

- Where will the resources for ministry-related activities come from?

What location or people group will benefit the most from this type of company? The holistic nature of a GCC means that it brings both material and spiritual benefits to a community. As we said before, the least-reached countries also tend to be the world's poorest. Many of the unreached are minority peoples who are victims of injustice and oppression. By bringing meaningful and dignified work to these communities, GCCs are engaging in an important ministry. For those employees who are Christian, an added benefit is the tithes that flow into the local church.

The value of a GCC is immeasurably greater when, in addition to the physiological and material benefits, it serves as a person's first meaningful point of contact with the gospel. This is most likely to occur if it is operating among large populations of people who have never heard about Jesus or have not seen the gospel's life-transforming message lived out in a practical way. There is no question that, while GCCs can certainly have an impact in highly evangelized parts of the world, the need is far greater in less-evangelized countries.

It also helps to think creatively about which stages of production—manufacturing, research and development, purchasing, marketing, customer service—can be located among those people and how the people can be most effectively engaged and mentored by the kingdom professionals. Cedric anticipates that the majority of his customers, at least initially, will be the treasury departments of less-developed countries. As part of the prioritizing process he should rank countries according to the magnitude of the counterfeiting problem and match that list against a list of the countries that have the greatest socioeconomic and spiritual needs. In the interest of getting the company up and running as quickly as possible, he will also want to consider contracting out the actual production of the ink, assuming he is comfortable that his technology can be protected. That way Cedric's company would be principally a marketing company with a network of agents and distributors, similar to Gateway Telecommunications Services (see chapter eleven).

What can this company do that other Christian organizations in the area cannot? While Christian organizations are permitted in most countries, they are closely watched in many cases to ensure that they are not clandestine efforts to do nothing more than evangelize and convert the nationals.

Many organizations comply with those restrictions and focus instead on such things as disaster relief and humanitarian assistance, the provision of medical care, teaching English, job training and other community services. These are all worthwhile and valid ministries, but there is a limit as to which segments of society can be reached by these methods and where these ministries can be located. By comparison, GCCs often have greater freedom and can reach an entirely different segment of society. For example, one kingdom professional recently shared how his business credentials enable him to build relationships with people he could never reach before as a traditional missionary. Specifically, local government or business leaders would have nothing to do with him as a missionary, but as the owner of a thriving business he now receives regular invitations to their homes and workplaces. This observation has been made countless times during our research, and it illustrates another important point about the strategic value of a GCC: the value of a missions strategy is greatest when the venture is reaching people that cannot be reached by other means.

Being associated with a foreign corporation can also give national Christians a stature and respect in society that they never enjoyed before. This is especially true when they hold positions of significant authority within the company. For example, one regional sales agent for Gateway Telecommunications Services is an active lay leader in the local church. Not only does his position provide much-needed income, both for his family and for his church, but his affiliation with a multinational corporation has enabled him to reach parts of his community that were formerly out of reach because of local prejudices.

Where will the resources for ministry-related activities come from? For those contemplating starting a GCC there is a natural desire to use company resources to fund ministries of every kind. Restraint is called for, however, for several reasons. First, as Tom Sudyk of Evangelistic Commerce often says, "A company that does not *focus* on making money will almost certainly never make any." The truth is, growing a company into one that can be consistently profitable is a monumental task, and siphoning money away from the company too early will make it even more challenging. A company is not likely to have a meaningful, long-term ministry impact if it fails. Therefore the first priority must be given to the company's survival. Some modest levels of corporate philanthropy may be acceptable, but in the early stages the tithes of the management team will probably be more significant.

Depending on the structure of the GCC, a careful distinction may also have to be made between the nonprofit and for-profit activities. While a for-profit corporation is free to do whatever it wishes with its profits (as long as the owners agree), a nonprofit corporation can only use its money for charitable purposes. GCCs that work in close partnership with nonprofit corporations must be careful to avoid the appearance that monies from the nonprofit are being used to benefit the for-profit company (and its owners). For example, in the past, some GCCs have been managed by people who are supported partially or entirely by donations made to mission agencies. While there are legal ways to structure such arrangements, not all relationships between GCCs and mission agencies are structured with the same care. The main thing to remember is that donations made to nonprofit corporations *can only be used for charitable purposes.* If a member of the management team receives some donor support for the charity work he or she does outside the company, so be it. But any work done for the company must be paid for by the company. Ignoring this can jeopardize the nonprofit's tax-exempt status, or worse, be prosecuted as a criminal act.

A counterargument is often made that people are more likely to pray for what they are supporting financially. Thus if we want to ensure that GCCs and their management teams have a solid foundation of prayer support, they should raise donor support. While there is some truth to this, we should not underestimate the ability of business professionals to build their own prayer support networks. As in several of the cases profiled in this book, often the business itself can be used as a means of getting and keeping people's attention. Some kingdom professionals have found other creative ways to solve this "prayer support requires donor support" conundrum. For example, the management team of a GCC in Southeast Asia draws full salaries from the company and also from donors. However, the donations are deposited in a separate, team-managed account for ministry purposes only. The team members therefore receive the benefit of regular prayer support but do not benefit financially from donations made to the ministry.

Some companies have reached a stage where they can devote significant resources toward orphanages, computer training centers and so on. Some GCCs will help facilitate visits from short-term ministry teams. For example, when the Silk Road Handicraft Company experienced a growth spurt, the founders wanted to promote some employees to supervisory positions but could not because those employees were unable to read and write sufficiently to perform those jobs. In response, the company hired a teacher—a kingdom professional—to teach reading and writing for six months. The company benefited, but more importantly, it also *paid* for the teacher. GCCs are in fact quite creative about finding ways to get "ministry leverage" out of their corporate resources. But as much as we would like to do away with the dichotomy between sacred and secular, care should always be taken when combining nonprofit and for-profit activities.

ASSEMBLE A MANAGEMENT TEAM

The most effective GCCs are those that are led by a qualified and balanced team of kingdom professionals. Each team member will naturally bring different skills and experiences, but they should all integrate their faith into every part of their daily life. Under no circumstances should someone who views business as a "cover" for ministry be accepted. Instead, team members should all see the business itself as a valid ministry.

Qualified candidates will be well grounded in the spiritual disciplines and have a history of drawing people's attention to Christ. There will be evidence of spiritual maturity and an active interest in helping others grow in their faith. Young Christians are not necessarily unfit for this work, but care should be taken to make sure they are properly supervised and discipled. It is important to remember that the principle purpose of GCCs, whether facilitative or pioneering, is to bring light into the darkest places—Satan's strongholds. Fierce spiritual opposition is guaranteed. Furthermore, there are unique temptations and trials involved in doing business in less-developed and religiously hostile countries that test the faith of even the strongest Christians. As a general rule, it is best for young believers or those who still need more business or ministry experience to begin working on those skills in a less challenging context first. Our research suggests that the old adage "experience is the best teacher" is absolutely true. It is also the best indicator of how effective a person will be on a GCC team.

For those who will be working crossculturally, additional skills are required, including language skills and an ability to adjust to a new culture (with its different styles of learning, decision-making, leadership, conflict resolution and so forth). Those who adapt most successfully tend to have a natural interest in establishing relationships with people from other cultures and exhibit an ability to share the gospel crossculturally as well. They are humble and can laugh at their own cultural mistakes. They are willing to adjust their lifestyle so that it does not inhibit their witness, and they treat the difficulties of living in a foreign country as challenges for growth rather than sources of irritation.

The necessary business experience will depend on the circumstances and the job being filled. Because the companies tend to be young and entrepreneurial in nature, the management team should consist of people who have experience working in similar situations. In other words, a person who has spent twenty years working in middle-level management for a large, hierarchical corporation may not be as suitable as someone who has worked for smaller (perhaps even defunct) companies. This does not mean, however, that team members must all be aggressive, type-A personalities. Successful team members come in every shape, size and personality type. What they do share, however, are passion, persistence, a capacity to learn from mistakes and a willingness to make decisions and take *calculated* risks. By that we mean they do not act recklessly, but neither do they allow themselves to become paralyzed by too much analysis and planning. They plan, pray and get advice. Then they act, and they do not obsess over what might have been.

The ideal team will include both expatriate and national believers who share similar values and vision. It is often necessary, even desirable, to have nonbelievers on the management team who can add strength in certain areas and, at least indirectly, enhance the prospects for effective ministry. When this is the case, care should be taken that no one is added who is hostile to the holistic ministry purpose of the company. Furthermore, if the company is going to reflect Christ in its community, it is essential that a substantial

THE IMPORTANCE OF TEAMS

A Great Commission Company that is both successful as a business and effective as a ministry requires more than an individual effort; it requires a team of men and women that reflects a balance of gifts, personalities and cultures. The importance of teamwork—working harmoniously together for the good of the whole—is pervasive in Scripture, as it is part of *missio Dei*, reflecting an important part of God's own Trinitarian nature. There are three reasons why strong and balanced teams are especially important in the context of a GCC.

1. Spiritual accountability and strength. Ecclesiastes 4:12 says that "A cord of three strands is not quickly broken." Such strength is especially important when trying to bring life and hope into the most spiritually oppressed parts of the world.

2. A persuasive testimony. The grace and forgiveness that teamwork requires can be a persuasive testimony, a model of God's own grace and unconditional love (Jn 13:35). This testimony is even more powerful when the team consists of people from different cultures. We see an example of this in Acts with the church in Antioch. David Shenk and Ervin Stutzman correctly point out that

> This congregation, made up of people from many different racial and ethnic backgrounds, led by persons from three continents, was unprecedented. This Antioch church was so unusual that the pagans gave them a nickname: Christians. . . . The multiracial and multiethnic leadership of this church was a persuasive testimony that God was indeed doing a new thing.[i]

THE IMPORTANCE OF TEAMS (Continued)

3. Synergy. A well-functioning team is synergistic; more can be achieved by working together than by working in an individualistic, uncoordinated fashion (1 Cor 12:4-31). For example, two fishermen are generally far more productive if they share a boat and split the tasks of fishing and piloting the boat than if they take separate boats.

It is noteworthy that Jesus always sent his disciples out in teams (Mk 6:7). Likewise, the apostle Paul always worked as part of a church planting team. A study of those teams is enlightening.[ii] First, we learn that some internal conflict is almost inevitable. For example, differences of opinion caused Paul and Barnabus's team to split up, although they continued leading other teams. Second, the most effective teams have at least one experienced member/leader. Third, the teams were almost always multicultural in composition. "It was important to Paul to have a cross-cultural team which included persons from the culture in which he intended to create churches."[iii]

The key to a successful GCC team is a commitment to God, to each other and to the task. Members must recognize, respect and enjoy the diversity of personalities and the variety of gifts and callings each member brings to the team.[iv]

[i] David W. Shenk and Ervin R. Stutzman, *Creating Communities of the Kingdom: New Testament Models of Church Planting* (Scottdale, Penn.: Herald Press, 1988), p. 44.

[ii] See Tom A. Steffen, *Passing the Baton: Church Planting That Empowers* (La Habra, Calif.: Center for Organizational and Ministry Development, 1997), pp. 58-59.

[iii] Shenk and Stutzman, *Creating Communities*, p. 47.

[iv] Adapted from Steffen, *Passing the Baton*.

share of those in key decision-making positions are kingdom professionals. (Unless stated otherwise, throughout this book "team member" refers to the Christian members of the management team.)

BUILD AN ADVISORY NETWORK

The most durable and effective GCCs have active participation and support from a wide range of advisers, from lawyers, accountants and technology experts to local government officials, mission agencies and leaders of the indigenous church. While not directly involved in the management of the company, these people can significantly improve the likelihood of success by helping identify obstacles and the strategies for overcoming them. They also bring access to a broad network of contacts and resources that the management teams may lack, including potential members of the team itself. The added credibility they give the venture, along with the network of relationships they represent, can help build broad-based support for the business/ ministry model, which is useful when trying to raise capital.

One study of successful business startups found that not only does an advisory network tend to accelerate the startup process, but those entrepreneurs with previous startup experience began developing these networks much earlier in the process than first-timers.[2] The most successful advice seekers followed these procedures:

- Identify people and organizations that will have an interest in the outcome of this project.

- Seek criticism, advice and suggestions from those people.

- Ask them for the names (at least two) of others who may be contacted, and get permission to use their names when doing so.

- Ask them what preparation is necessary before speaking to those contacts.

- Do the necessary preparation.

- Return later to the original contacts and tell them how their advice helped, thus cementing useful relationships.

- Repeat these steps for the new sets of contacts.

A common mistake is to rely too heavily on the provision of free or sharply discounted services. Many people are indeed happy to provide discounts, but care should be taken, especially with professional services such as legal or accounting help, not to rely exclusively on those who offer the cheapest rates. The danger is that a "volunteer mentality" may take hold whereby they view the GCC more as a hobby than a client. This can mean settling for help from people working outside their area of specialty, or waiting while they take care of their higher-paying clients first. Like any business, a GCC should be prepared to pay market rates for these services or work out some agreeable alternative.

Another cautionary reminder, especially for those with extensive experience in the nonprofit world, is that some questions and some risks will inevitably remain. That is the nature of entrepreneurship. Quite frankly, the only way some answers will ever be known is to try it and find out. Therefore, while we encourage the active participation and support of many advisers, one must guard against making the decision-making process too unwieldy. A committee mentality will paralyze the planning process.

DEVELOP A BUSINESS PLAN

At some point somebody will ask to see a business plan. Not that business plans are necessarily the best predictors of success, but they at least demonstrate that you have done your homework. The business plan should succinctly describe the opportunity, identify the strengths and weaknesses of the business model and the management team, and give some conservative estimates about how and when the venture will break even. Prospective investors will naturally want to see a business plan, but so will others who are being asked to make substantial commitments, such as advisers and prospective members of the management team. Entrepreneurs often resent the exercise of writing a business plan, but there is frankly no better way to prepare for what Harvard business professor William Sahlman calls "the most daunting journey of a businessperson's career."[3] Moreover, because the management team cannot be everywhere at once, having a business plan that can be sent to interested parties is an efficient way to make initial introductions and to sort out the seriously interested from the merely curious.

Most business plans, says Sahlman, "waste too much ink on numbers and devote too little to the information that really matters to intelligent investors"[4] They put too much effort into making financial projections that everyone knows are little more than blind guesses and are overly optimistic about the amount of time, effort and capital that will be required to achieve profitability. Instead Sahlman maintains that the best business plans illuminate the following:

- **The people.** The men and women starting and running the venture, as well as the outside parties providing key services or important resources for it, such as its lawyers, accountants and suppliers. Ideally there is an energetic managerial team in place with skills and experiences directly relevant to the opportunity they are pursuing. It is best if they have also worked successfully together in the past.

- **The opportunity.** A profile of the business itself: what it will sell and to whom, whether the business can grow and how fast, what its economics are, who and what stand in the way of success. The business model is attractive and sustainable, and can create and defend a competitive edge. Many options exist for expanding the scale and scope of the business, and these options are unique to the enterprise and its team.

- **The context.** The big picture—the regulatory, demographic and macroeconomic environments. While these things cannot be controlled, are they at least favorable?

- **The risk and reward.** An assessment of everything that can go wrong and right, and a discussion of how the management team can mitigate the impact of difficult events.

In the end, great businesses "have attributes that are easy to identify but hard to assemble."[5] By focusing on these key areas, the business plan can give the reader confidence that the obstacles have been carefully considered and that a plan is in place for overcoming them.

DEVELOP A GREAT COMMISSION PLAN

Some stakeholders will naturally be more interested in and more skilled at evaluating the missions opportunity than the business plan. Therefore it also makes good sense to write a Great Commission plan. This will highlight many of the same things as the business plan.

- **The people.** The kingdom professionals on the team are all committed to the ministry goals of the company. Non-Christians at the management level are not opposed to those goals. Where the team is weak in terms of ministry experience or skills, outside parties have agreed to fill in the gaps. Ideally each team member will have a history of working successfully in this context.

- **The opportunity.** The founders know what they are hoping to accomplish and why. The goals are clear and measurable, albeit not always perfectly. Ideally the company will open up opportunities that did not exist before or reach a segment of society that was difficult to reach before. The ministry can be sustained with local resources, so it does not require the long-term involvement of foreigners.

- **The context.** The big picture—the socioeconomic and religious environment in this country or among this people group. The status of the church.

- **The risk and reward.** How difficult is it for local Christians to express their faith freely? How difficult will it be to openly pursue ministry in this country? Is it possible for the ministry to create problems for the business?

The failure to achieve the highly publicized goal of "a church for every people by the year 2000" has created a kind of planning backlash among some in the ministry community. Yet even those who are the most critical of what they see as excessive planning do not pursue ministry haphazardly. It is basic good stewardship to have at least some idea of what we are trying to do and why. The Great Commission plan helps bring clarity to the process.

ASSESSING THE VIABILITY OF A GCC

The following are just a few of the questions that should be asked when assessing the viability of a GCC.

Economic Viability

1. Is there a clear statement of the purpose and goals for the company?

2. Does the management team have the appropriate experience and training?

3. Can the business create and maintain a competitive advantage?

4. From a financial perspective, is the business an attractive investment?

5. Is there a clear path from startup to financial sustainability?

6. Are there investors and other advisers committed to helping the company reach financial sustainability?

7. Is this a business concept that has worked in other contexts?

8. What are the risks?

9. Is the business model flexible enough to allow for expansion, changes in direction, or alliances with other companies?

10. How will the net earnings be distributed?

11. How and when can the investors expect to be repaid?

ASSESSING THE VIABILITY OF A GCC
(Continued)

Missional Viability

1. Is the business concept consistent with the missional focus and objectives?

2. Is there adequate potential for making a significant kingdom impact?

3. Does the company have a multicultural, multigenerational team of kingdom professionals in place that has a track record of effective ministry inside and outside the workplace?

4. Has the management team identified other mission organizations working in the area, and are they open to partnering with them?

5. Does the plan demonstrate an understanding and respect for the legal and ethical boundaries between for-profit and nonprofit activities?

6. Does the business create socially beneficial "backward linkages" with local firms?

7. Is the net impact on the host economy's balance of payments positive?

8. Is there a plan to turn over as much authority and responsibility as possible (missions and business) to local professionals?

9. Is the management team committed to serving under the local church (if one exists)?

10. Is the management team committed to communicating regularly with other stakeholders so that they know how to pray and know what things they can do to benefit the work (for example, short-term trips)?

6
SUSTAINING SUCCESS

It is not what a man does that determines whether his work is sacred or secular, it is why he does it.

A. W. TOZER

Successfully drafting a plan and recruiting a team is a significant accomplishment. But the biggest challenges are still ahead. Sometimes the challenge is external, such as an unexpected change in the business climate. Other times the challenge comes from within the organization, such as when the business and ministry teams (if divided into two groups) feel disconnected from one another, leading to frustrations, mistakes and even failure of the entire enterprise. In this chapter we will focus mainly on internal challenges and on how GCCs can be structured and governed to minimize those challenges. We will begin by identifying the stakeholders—those who have an interest in the success of a GCC—and the contributions each can make. Then we will discuss the ownership and governance of GCCs. If done well, the governance process can solidify the commitment of the stakeholders and take some of the burden off the management team. If done poorly, it can be a tremendous burden. The primary purpose of this chapter is to suggest how the stakeholder relationships can be managed for maximum effectiveness.

GCC STAKEHOLDERS
As we said before, a successful and effective GCC requires more than an individual effort. It requires a team of qualified men and women that is focused on that task. Collectively we will refer to this team as "stakeholders," those who have an interest in the success of a GCC. They include the own-

ers, management team, home churches, mission agencies, advisers, indigenous church (if one exists) and local community. (Many of these will have already been part of the planning process.) Some stakeholders will naturally be more attentive to the business concerns and others to the ministry concerns. For this reason we must begin by identifying these people, their interests and the contributions they each make to the overall enterprise.

Management team. The first and probably most obvious stakeholders are the kingdom professionals who make up the management team. If a company is going to reflect Christ in its community, it is essential that those in key decision-making positions be committed to that goal. The qualifications and training of each member will naturally vary somewhat depending on their position in the company. In addition, those living and working in a crosscultural setting should have some experience and training in ministering crossculturally. In many cases these are people who quit higher paying and more prestigious jobs for the opportunity to participate in the challenging and exciting work of the GCC. This complete commitment to the company is one of their chief strengths, but it can also be a weakness if they dismiss the help of others who have not made a similar commitment.

Investors. Few entrepreneurs have the financial resources necessary to build a company from start to finish. A GCC will almost certainly require outside financing—money provided by someone outside the immediate management team. In the Christian missions world this money is occasionally raised through donations, but those are exceptional cases because GCCs do not enjoy the tax exemption of nonprofit organizations. The more typical approach is to raise capital through loans or by selling an equity stake in the company. Raising serious money usually requires allowing the investors to play an active role in the company. Such investors will typically insist on regular reports, one or more seats on the board of directors and even the right to appoint or fire members of the management team. In return the business receives not only financial capital (usually meted out in stages) but also an experienced and savvy consultant who brings a long and impressive track record in business. They often have extensive connections with lawyers, investment bankers and so forth that are essential for growing a company. However, such successful track records often come with a "grow fast" mentality that can sometimes be at odds with the missional goals of the company.

Home church. Home churches are an important resource for GCCs, as the pews are full of people who would love to assist on a short- or long-term basis. Once engaged and feeling a sense of ownership, these laypeople often bring a seemingly limitless amount of creative energy, and many will put a great deal of time, energy and money into the effort. Furthermore, once they have been exposed to the ways God is using business professionals in other places, they gain a better appreciation for the impact they can have in their own workplace. However, to the degree that they lack international business experience, they sometimes approach it with an overly simplistic view about how businesses work in other parts of the world and how difficult it can be to succeed in those environments.

Mission agencies. Agencies have an important role to play in the work of GCCs. Agencies bring years of experience and a single-minded focus on missions that most home churches lack. They understand better than anyone the cultures and worldviews that are embedded in the regions in which the company operates. In addition they have their own networks of supporters, consultants and other resources that can help the GCC accomplish both its ministry and its business goals. For example, former missionaries have been known to make highly effective human resource managers because of their language skills and crosscultural people skills. Agencies can also help coordinate the work of the GCC with other ministries in the area and help screen and train kingdom professionals who wish to join the management team. The downside is that people in the missions world easily forget or downplay the importance of the GCC's business success. As specialists in understanding different cultures, they sometimes struggle most at understanding the culture of business. Moreover their background in the nonprofit world and its donor culture makes it difficult for them to appreciate that corporate managers are legally and morally obligated to make an honest effort at *returning* money that has been invested in the company, ideally with a fair rate of return.

Advisers. Other resources that are critical to a GCC's success include the services of lawyers, bankers, accountants, consultants, technology experts and so on. Again, like any business, a GCC should be prepared to pay market rates for these services or to work out an alternative such as stock or stock options.

Indigenous church. If a church already exists in the community of interest, the GCC needs to view itself first and foremost as a *servant* of that church. Being a trusted and valued member of the local ministry team is one of the greatest privileges of being involved with a GCC. The local Christians can also be an infinitely valuable resource for the company, given their insider knowledge of the culture, language, regulations and so forth.

Community. Finally, the local community—including customers, suppliers, employees and the local government—has an interest in seeing the GCC succeed. In fact, there is a direct relationship between the help one can expect from the local community and the visible benefits the GCC brings to the community. More often than not, those businesses that are harassed by government officials bring the fewest benefits to the community. When properly managed, a GCC will help raise up new entrepreneurs in the community, stimulating new businesses that become new sources of economic activity, jobs and witness.

THE UNIQUE ROLE OF THE CHIEF EXECUTIVE OFFICER

One of the key responsibilities of the chief executive officer (CEO) will be to act as the liaison between the management team and the other stakeholders. Because every stakeholder relationship is costly in terms of time, energy and other resources, one of the most important parts of the CEO's job will be to cultivate and manage the optimal number of these relationships. In the planning stage some advisers undoubtedly contributed more than others, and some may have unwittingly been more burdensome than helpful (for example, by being overly zealous or overly critical). Thus, now is a good time to evaluate the future of those relationships. We suggest a two-tiered approach similar to what many nonprofit boards use. That is, the CEO should maintain close ties with a small group of stakeholders (akin to an "executive committee") who can meet the majority of the needs of the company and can respond quickly to those needs. Other stakeholders can expect to be contacted regularly, but less frequently.

Another issue unique to the CEO is whether that person should also be the leader of the ministry team or whether GCCs work better when the leadership of the "business" and the "ministry" are separated. On this matter there are sharp differences of opinion. On one hand, there are those who are uncomfortable with the implied dichotomization. If these are truly holistic, integrated enterprises, it should be difficult, if not impossible, to distinguish between the business and the ministry. Indeed many times it is. But there are also times when some level of distinction needs to be made between the for-profit activities and the nonprofit activities, if only for legal reasons. Those who advocate the separate leadership approach maintain that this is the only way to ensure that both tasks receive the appropriate attention, and that this approach helps minimize the confusion that can occur when the boss is also perceived as the spiritual leader/discipler. Opponents of this approach are equally convinced that unless the same person leads both the business and the ministry, the GCC can take on a split personality of sorts, or get pulled in two separate directions, jeopardizing the profitability goals, the ministry goals or both.

The two approaches are not necessarily contradictory. Instead, they point to what we believe is the best solution of all: to have an active board of directors that is representative of all the stakeholders and committed to the holistic purpose of the company. Ultimately the board should be the "keeper of the flame" and should hold the management team accountable to the goals set out in the business plan and the Great Commission plan. The specific leadership needs will vary according to those plans. For some GCCs, such as Pura Vida Coffee (see chapter nine), it makes good sense to have one team leader—the CEO—focusing primarily on the business (in the United States, in their case) and another leader focusing on the ministry (in Costa Rica, in their case). In situations when such a sharp distinction between business and ministry is not possible, the CEO often oversees both efforts. But in either case, the board has the ultimate responsibility of making sure the company stays on course. The truth is, no matter how determined a person is to treat the business and ministry as an integrated whole, the intentionality of a GCC implies that, from time to time, tough choices will need to be made between the business and the ministry. Even the most experienced kingdom professionals can benefit from the wise and timely counsel of a board of directors.

This raises another issue about the CEO. While it is true that this person must be able to manage the stakeholders and prevent those relationships from becoming a burden, the CEO must also be willing, ultimately, to submit to those same stakeholders when they are acting collectively as a board of directors. Put another way, the CEO must avoid getting pulled in separate directions by individual stakeholders or board members for the sake of their own agendas. But when the stakeholders are speaking with one voice as a board, the CEO must have the temperament necessary to accept and submit to that counsel.

GOVERNING THE GREAT COMMISSION COMPANY

Until recently few people outside academia cared about the seemingly arcane topic of corporate governance. However, recent corporate scandals and bankruptcies involving such high-profile firms as Enron, WorldCom and KMart have changed all that. In theory, corporations are managed in the owners' (the stockholders) best interest, with the board of directors keeping the upper-level management team honest and accountable. In practice this oversight and accountability can break down and create opportunities for misconduct and fraud. There are now some widely recognized principles of good governance, and thanks in part to the recent scandals, many corporations are taking those principles seriously for the first time. These include making sure that the board can act with a measure of independence, that it is not "stacked" too heavily in favor of the management team, and that board members have a stake in the outcome (some "skin in the game," so to speak). The aim is to have a board that will put the *company's* interest above that of the individual members of the management team.

The missional purpose of a GCC adds a layer of complexity to the problem that has not been given much attention. One thing we can say with confidence is that GCCs have generally been governed very loosely, either because the managers own all of the outstanding shares in the company or because the investors "trust the managers' heart." With this culture of slack oversight (combined with the naive reluctance to offer returns that are commensurate to the risk) it is not surprising that GCCs typically have trouble raising substantial sums of capital. Changing this culture will require a paradigm shift for many stakeholders. Specifically, the missions community needs to start treating these as legitimate business opportunities rather than as clever disguises for professional missionaries, and the business community needs to start compensating the missions stakeholders for the essential contributions they make to the overall effort. This appreciation for each other's contribution should be reflected in the board. The following questions will help identify the key issues:

- Who should sit on the board?
- What are the roles and responsibilities of the board?
- How should the board be organized for optimal performance?

Who should sit on the board? The short answer to this question is, the owners. But who are the owners of a GCC? To answer this question, let us return to our friend Cedric from chapter five. When he started his ink company all he brought to the table was an idea and a relatively small amount of money. Yet that idea was a significant, albeit intangible, contribution to the business. Indeed there would be no business without it. Similarly, the company is also the product of the significant, intangible contribution of his partner, who was essential in taking the idea and making it into a potentially viable business. Finally, there were those who contributed money and other resources along the way. When all is said and done, they will all own a stake in the company, and those stakes will reflect the value of the intangible as well as the tangible investments. The point here is that intangible assets have real value and are routinely factored into the value of individual ownership stakes.

Now consider the GCC. Does not a similar argument apply when talking about the intangible investments of mission agencies, churches or other stakeholders? We have talked about the need for the missions community to think differently, now it is the business community's turn to be challenged. If the founders are truly serious about sustaining the vision for the company and serving Christ's interests rather than their own, they will not only seek the help of like-minded stakeholders but also invite them to serve on the board and submit themselves to the board's leadership. Those board members, in turn, need to have a stake in the company, some "skin in the game." This stake may be assigned to them individually or to the organization(s) they represent, but one way or another the stake should be real, and each board member needs to feel the inevitable tension between more profitability and more ministry.[1]

Board members should be people who can serve as the liaison between the GCC and the stakeholders they represent. Ideally they will have the authority to make decisions on behalf of those stakeholders and have the clout to persuade the stakeholders to take action when necessary. Other useful people to have on the board are those who can connect the company to potentially large customers, help solve recurring financial or legal problems, or simply add to the company's credibility. Ultimately the board should be representative of many, if not all, the stakeholders, and everyone should be committed to the vision and goals of the company. They should be willing to set their individual relationships and agendas aside and make decisions that are in the best interest of the overall enterprise, even if it gets uncomfortable.

What are the roles and responsibilities of the board? The key to good governance is striking a balance between too much and too little control. Too much control can backfire by stifling creativity and slowing down the decision-making process. Too little control encourages laziness or mischief. Instead everyone should understand and agree to the purpose of the company and the proper role of the board. Furthermore, board members should understand their specific role, be provided with the authority and tools to fill that role, and be held accountable for their actions. Following are some of the things a board will be expected to do:

- *Strategic planning.* The board should regularly review and update the business plan and Great Commission plan for the company.

- *Key hiring decisions.* By the time a board of directors is constituted, many of the key players will already be in place. Still there will almost certainly be gaps in the management team, and the board should be willing to use its extensive network of contacts to find suitable candidates. Furthermore, if the CEO or another member of the management team is failing to fulfill the objectives set out by the board and reasonable attempts to rectify the problem have failed, then it is the responsibility of the board to make the necessary changes.

- *Key financial decisions.* The board should be involved in financial decisions that can impact the long-term viability of the business or its ministry. These include raising additional capital, authorizing major capital
  expenditures, signing long-term financial commitments, mergers, alliances and management compensation packages. At the same time, however, the management team should be given as much latitude as possible
  to run the day-to-day operations as it sees fit.

- *Vision maintenance.* Without a steady flow of information about the *ministry* impact of the business, stakeholders may lose interest or forget to
  pray. The board should ensure that the appropriate level of communication is maintained. This includes newsletters to stakeholders, hosting visits by stakeholders, being an advocate for the company in churches and
  conferences, coordinating visits from short-term ministry teams and so
  on. In the case of facilitative GCCs, the management team itself should
  take regular trips to "the field" and budget these trips as part of the cost
  of doing business. Pura Vida Coffee and Homestead Partners are two excellent examples of companies doing that.

Finally, board members can also expect to be asked to do things like provide expert advice on important questions (legal, financial or missional
questions, for example), serve as mentors to the management or staff, or
help identify customers or opportunities for alliances. In short, board members are every bit a part of the GCC team, and only those who can commit
the time and energy necessary should consider accepting such an invitation.

How should the board be organized for optimal performance? Many of
the responsibilities outlined above are routine or recurring in nature. In
those cases the board may want to establish committees that are given the
authority to act on behalf of the board. In addition to streamlining the governance process, committees can also be a way of encouraging the participation of non-board members and cultivating potential new board members. Committees that are chaired by a board member but open to non-
board members are essentially a variation of the two-tiered approach to
managing stakeholders mentioned above. Following are some potential
committees:

- *Finance and audit committee.* This committee will be responsible for ongoing financial review and will evaluate proposals that have significant financial implications. It will also develop and regularly update company guidelines that will help the management team avoid legal problems that can occur when working in partnership with nonprofit organizations.

- *Missions (or Great Commission) audit committee.* This committee will take primary responsibility for evaluating the ministry effectiveness of the company. It will regularly review and update (if necessary) the Great Commission plan. It will also work with the financial audit committee when financial proposals have potentially significant ministry implications. It will also help raise funds for the nonprofit activities associated with the company.

- *Investor and stakeholder relations.* This committee will ensure that investors and other stakeholders are kept informed, including preparing the monthly or quarterly financial reports. It will also help coordinate visits from advisers or short-term ministry teams.

- *Personnel committee.* This committee will oversee the recruiting and screening of members of the management team. It will be the one primarily responsible for evaluating the CEO's performance and developing and updating company policies regarding compensation, benefits, performance reviews and so on.

Depending on the specific context, there are many other issues that occur routinely enough—technology and legal questions, for example—to justify forming a committee. The purpose is not to create a bureaucracy but to streamline the governance process. Each committee should understand its purpose, be empowered to make decisions and be held accountable for its actions.

In summary, the most consistently effective GCCs are those that are governed by a like-minded board of directors. While the board should consist of people who believe in the management team and its vision for the company, it should not be beholden to the management. An effective board must be able and willing to make tough choices if necessary. The board as a whole, as well as the committees, should be able to meet independently, without the

CEO being present. Furthermore, the CEO should not also be the chairman of the board, as that makes it difficult for the board to act contrary to the CEO's wishes. CEOs who hold both titles are, in effect, signaling their unwillingness to submit to a board of directors. There may be no better way to test a CEO's willingness to be submissive than to see if he or she is willing to let someone else lead the board.

QUESTIONS FOR REVIEW

1. In which stakeholder category do you think you best fit? Is it possible to be in more than one category?

2. What is your opinion about maintaining separate leadership for the business and ministry? Does your answer depend on the size of the company? Its location? Its business or ministry strategy?

3. Do you think a board of directors is a good idea for all GCCs? Does your answer depend on the size of the company? Its location? Its business or ministry strategy?

4. Do you think all stakeholders should be shareholders? What other ways can a GCC's interest be aligned with a stakeholder's, and vice versa?

PART TWO

GREAT COMMISSION COMPANIES IN PRACTICE

The purpose of part one was to give the economic, historical and theological context for Great Commission Companies and to identify the key issues related to starting and governing a GCC. Everything we have said thus far reflects the "ideal," not the actual, GCC. We are now ready to look more closely at some actual examples. As we will see, each company is unique and reflects a slightly different vision of what a GCC should be. We chose these companies not because they are perfect but because they illustrate some different approaches and important points we have made along the way.

Unfortunately, we live in an age when there is a great deal of hostility toward Christian missions. For this reason we use pseudonyms for most people and companies and avoid many specific details. Some readers may wish for more details. But we have discovered that far more important than the business itself is the *people* behind the business—their personal spiritual development, their prior experiences in ministry and business, and so on. Thus the following chapters were written in a more narrative, biographical style. The stories illustrate the marvelous ways God draws people to himself and prepares them for ministry. We hope you enjoy these stories as much as we did.

7

THE INDEPENDENT, PIONEERING GCC

SILK ROAD HANDICRAFT COMPANY

ESTABLISHED: 1988

LOCATION: Farstan

EMPLOYEES: Roughly three hundred between two factories

PROJECTED REVENUE (2003): $3.1 million

MISSION STATEMENT: To make money, to build people, and to create eternal value.

OVERVIEW

The Silk Road Handicraft Company is a maker of handcrafted home furnishings. Some product lines are sold in high-end retail stores such as the Expo Design Center, and others are sold through retail outlets such as Hallmark Stores and the television station QVC. The company was founded by Jeff and Silvia Nolan (not their real names) in 1988. Their business backgrounds were not particularly strong at the time, but what they lacked in experience they made up for in prayer, faith and hard work. Today the company has two factories in Farstan, which employ a total of about three hundred people. Roughly 90 percent of the employees are now Christian, but the more exciting story has to do with the impact these employees are having outside the factory. Not only are many friends and family members also hearing about and accepting Christ, but a core group of about two dozen people are now committed to spreading that transforming message throughout their community—a densely populated village plagued by problems stemming from gambling, witchcraft, prostitution and so on. To date, eight churches have been planted, varying in size from twelve to four hundred people.

PERSONAL BACKGROUND

Jeff was born into a non-Christian home where Christ was essentially a non-issue. In 1968 he joined the Navy and, while stationed in northern California, met a group of people who had an indescribably attractive quality about them. He remembers thinking, "I don't know what they have, but whatever it is, I want it." It was not long before he accepted their invitation to attend church and, ultimately, accepted Christ as his personal Savior. He has been serious about living out his faith ever since. For example, soon after accepting Christ he began teaching a weekly Sunday school class on the Navy base. As a new believer with little knowledge of the Bible, he "prepared" his lessons by first attending the Sunday morning worship service at Peninsula Bible Church, then rushing back to base in time to deliver the same lesson there. He also began reaching out to the drug users in his barracks, but this proved to be a more challenging ministry because the guys distrusted this squeaky clean do-gooder. Even some of his Christian sailor buddies thought he was overdoing things a bit.

Undaunted and sincere about his desire to help drug addicts and alcoholics find the true source of fulfillment, he brought this problem before the Lord. The reply was: "You're with them, but you don't love them." This began what has become a lifelong process of learning how to love others. He discovered that being active in ministry is not the same thing as loving the people he is ministering to. He responded by listening more and talking less, spending quality time with the guys and developing genuine, caring relationships with them. Greater success soon followed.

Jeff was eventually transferred overseas, an experience that forced him to learn how to feed himself spiritually. He experimented with different styles of personal devotions and worship, even going so far as to conduct a full-length worship service by himself in the woods. It was an awkward, difficult period for this young believer, but eventually he settled into a routine that included spending two hours every night—from 10:00 p.m. to midnight—at a nearby track field in quiet communion with the Lord. During this time he learned not just how to talk to God, but more important, how to *listen*. It was during this yearlong assignment, and in particular during a short trip to the nearby country of Nearstan, that the Lord began revealing to Jeff his calling to central Asia.

After the Navy, Jeff enrolled in college, where he majored in philosophy and minored in Russian. During college he poured himself into a wide variety of ministries including evangelistic Bible studies and outreaches to the high schools and local parks. It was during one of the Bible studies that he first met Silvia, a beautiful young woman with a Roman Catholic background. Silvia dropped in to talk to a friend of hers about a disturbing letter she had received from her sister. The letter described her sister's recent "born again" experience, and Silvia, concerned that her sister had joined a cult, needed someone to help her make sense of the strange letter. Jeff and the two women discussed the basics of salvation into the wee hours of the night, and Jeff continued the dialogue the next day. By then the main thing keeping Silvia from allowing Christ to be Lord of her life was that she somehow knew God would make her serve in Africa as a missionary. In retrospect they laugh about it, but at the time they had no idea they would one day be married and serving Christ in Farstan. How Jeff helped her resolve this fear is a good illustration of how he views obedience—something that is not burdensome but instead is the secret to experiencing life's greatest fulfillment and joy. In a very gentle and thoughtful way, he proceeded.

Jeff: "Do you believe that God *knows* you better than anyone on this earth knows you, better than you even know yourself?"

Silvia: "Yes."

Jeff: "Do you believe that God *loves* you better than anyone on this earth loves you, better than you even love yourself?"

Silvia: "Yes."

Jeff: "Well if he *knows* you and *loves* you more than anyone else, then even if hypothetically he sent you to Africa, don't you think it would be because serving him in Africa is what would make you the most happy?"

This not only removed the last obstacle to her accepting Christ but also marked the beginning of their life and ministry together. After graduation they married and joined a Russo-American church where Jeff served as an assistant pastor until leaving to attend seminary. After seminary they moved to Tennessee and pastored a church for two years before deciding that the pastoral calling requires certain administrative gifts that Jeff does not possess. He is gifted in teaching and discipleship, but he feels better suited for less-formal ministry roles.

This explains how this seminary-trained philosopher ended up starting his own business making waterbed frames in 1981. While some might see this as a career change, a more apt description would be a change in *venue*. His central passion—the reason he still got out of bed every morning—was to serve Christ and to do things that would advance his kingdom. Jeff's "flock" was the customers, suppliers, coworkers and strangers he interacted with every day. It was not long before he had a Bible study going, which quickly became two Bible studies, then three—a growth rate of about four to five people per week until his ministry reached a steady state of about 150 people. (All told, he estimates that he helped disciple about one thousand people through that ministry.) He had no church-planting aspirations but instead encouraged these people to attend and contribute to their own churches. Nevertheless, the pressure to start a church grew, and a compromise was eventually struck: the leaders of the group quietly incorporated it as a religious nonprofit organization, and he agreed that as long as sufficient income came in each month, he would make this informal discipleship and teaching ministry his full-time occupation.

About seven years later the Soviet Union started unraveling and the Farstan government began allowing American families into the country. The Nolan family recognized this as the opportunity they had been preparing for, and with the blessing and temporary financial support of their "church" in Tennessee, they moved to Farstan.

COMPANY HISTORY

Once in the country, the first thing they had to do was become more proficient in the local language. Their plan was to attend language classes for two years, then find a job with a multinational corporation. Two months into the language classes, however, the government announced it would start allowing wholly foreign-owned companies into the country, and Jeff decided to submit the necessary paperwork. He expected the approval process to take a year or more, like everything else seemingly did in this country. To his utter amazement, the application was approved in thirty days. This was a mixed blessing, however, because while the change in his visa status—from student to businessman—gave them the permission they were seeking to move off campus, it also required them to withdraw from language school.

Jeff is, well, philosophical about this experience, maintaining that followers of Christ must have "a sense of anticipation" because Christ will regularly take them out of their comfort zone and force them into situations where they must depend on his strength alone. Ready or not, the Nolan family was now squarely in the middle of one of those situations. Under the circumstances, it is hard to blame Jeff if the business was not very well conceived in the beginning.

The personal burden period (1988-1993). Farstan was hoping to attract two types of foreign companies: technology-intensive businesses that could help the country modernize and labor-intensive businesses that could commit to exporting 100 percent of their production. Jeff opted for the latter. Beyond that, he had little idea what to do. The only other goal he had was to stay small. "We knew we would be making mistakes every day," he recalls, "and as a small company the mistakes [such as hiring a purchasing manager who embezzled five thousand dollars] would be less painful."

This is when a friend—a fly-fishing enthusiast—suggested that he make and export hand-tied fishing flies. The friend promised to take care of the marketing side of the business in the United States and backed up that promise by providing materials and money to help Jeff get started (ten thousand dollars in combined value). Under the circumstances this seemed like a reasonable idea, so Jeff rented a seven-hundred-square-foot shop and hired a Farstan manager along with four workers. With few questions asked, Jeff shipped the product back to his friend in the States, who was in fact making little effort to sell anything. Instead, he merely paid Jeff for the shipment and accumulated fishing flies. Before Jeff had a chance to remedy this problem, his friend and only customer died. So ended Jeff's first, but not last, experience with being dependent on a single customer.

Jeff began looking into other business ideas, and in the process he started learning how to make home furnishings. The products he made were so beautifully crafted that an American acquaintance assured him that he could sell as much as Jeff could make. Jeff admits that he was easily excited by these kinds of grandiose statements in the early days but is much more skeptical about them now. The man flew out for a visit and the two began working out the details of the partnership. However, as the realities of the unsettled political and economic atmosphere began to sink in, his enthusiastic friend not only lost interest in the business but literally had to be evacuated from the country because he was bordering on a nervous breakdown.

The political and economic crisis that quickly followed forced Jeff into a survival mode of sorts in which he had little choice but to buy and sell in the local market. In the process he learned how to build and maintain his own equipment, and he identified the most reliable sources for raw materials. However, while relying exclusively on local resources may have been good for the local economy, it also demonstrated to everybody that there were no proprietary technologies or skills required to do what he was doing. In other words, there was little to prevent others from competing against him. More than a few employees left his company over the next few years and became direct competitors. In fact he now wonders, only half jokingly, whether a better business strategy might have been to become a training facility or to sell franchises.

There was one distinction, however, that was difficult for his competitors to replicate. That was the reputation he built for high-quality work. In Farstan, as in many other countries where the link between effort and reward has become a foreign concept, something in the culture tends to inhibit the production of consistently high-quality goods or services. This problem is arguably one of the biggest obstacles many developing countries face in becoming competitive in the global markets. For this reason, quality is usually the first and most important problem foreign companies must solve when they locate a factory in a developing country.

Many kingdom professionals have found that there is no better place to start the discipling process than in this area. Employees must be taught that under no circumstances are the deception and pride at the root of the quality problem acceptable. Jeff has made it clear that, as one who is committed to following Jesus, his company will treat every customer as if he or she were Jesus Christ. "Poor-quality work brings shame on the company as well as the country and is therefore better off thrown away than sold," he says. To reinforce this point he has been known to smash defective product in front of startled employees. The message has sunk in. Today it is not uncommon to hear the same smashing sound being made by employees. Keep in mind that the employees are paid by the piece, so it takes no small amount of discipline to smash a piece and start over. Jeff also will impose penalties when necessary. He maintains that, as a matter of biblical principle, "people need to know there are consequences to their actions." For example, the work teams are not paid for product that does not pass inspection, and if anyone tries to slip shoddy product past the inspection process, more severe penalties are imposed.

Jeff soon met a man from eastern Europe who produced beautiful, labor-intensive home furnishings. The two formed a business relationship in which the man taught Jeff the techniques and provided the materials, and Jeff oversaw the production side of the business. For his part Jeff received a fixed rate per unit produced, and his profits were based on his ability to produce it for less.[1] This began a period of dramatic growth for the company, not only in terms of revenues and employees (it now had 120 employees working in a 12,000-square-foot factory), but also in terms of its core competencies.

Things went reasonably well until one of their employees—the company driver—began having a clandestine affair with the business partner. (Jeff and Silvia suspect that the woman was motivated by a desire to manage her own factory.) Not long after the affair started, the man divorced his wife, married the younger woman, set up a competing factory and began recruiting Jeff's employees. This part of their scheme failed, however, because the employees, recognizing that Jeff was a man of integrity and fairness, chose to stay. Nevertheless, the business relationship, not to mention Jeff's only customer, was now history.

Jeff refers to these early years as the personal burden period because any progress they would see, either spiritually or with the business, came with great difficulty. "We were learning to draw on God, but not for the right things," he says. Month after month they were seeing miraculous answers to prayer as they were trusting God to bail them out of problems, but they were not "trusting him to run the business," and as a result, they were making precious little progress.

The personal growth period (1994-1997). Rather than compete against his former partner, Jeff responded to the betrayal by turning his attention to developing new products and finding new customers. These too were very artistic products aimed for the collectibles market. The products were immediately picked up by the television shopping channel QVC and retailers such as Hallmark. In fact, the response exceeded his wildest expectations, and he was quickly overwhelmed by the demand, a critical mistake that forced his customers to look for other sources. His competitors turned out to be not only more skilled and resourceful, but they also introduced lower-priced versions of the products and thus seized an even larger part of the market. Jeff managed to hang on to a small share of the high-end market, but his company has never been more than a marginal player in this market ever since.

Yet in spite of his continued struggles with the business, Jeff refers to this as the beginning of the personal growth period, a time when "self began getting out of the way" and the management team started allowing God to lead the company. The change started when the core management team received a strong impression from the Lord—each within a forty-eight-hour period—that it was time to start praying together, specifically *for the business.* They came to realize that the business and its employees are some of the "talents" for which they will one day be asked to give an account (see Mt 25:14-30). Until then they viewed the business primarily as a source of income, not as something God actually cared about. This prompted them to make prayer "organic to the company" by taking everything—machinery problems, personnel problems, cash-flow problems and every employee—before the Lord. In the process they discovered that "God is quite comfortable with business." They started to see remarkable changes in the atmosphere of the company and in the way problems were handled. They also began to see in a fresh way that God was not just interested in the people's souls but also truly interested in the business itself.

We should add that they were also seeing conversions—on average about two or three per week, sometimes as many as thirty. Jeff and Silvia claim very little credit for this because, the truth is, the evangelizing was almost exclusively the result of worker-to-worker relationships. The Nolans were aware of what was happening, but they were never directly involved. The employees recall things differently, however. From their perspective God had clearly sent the Nolans, and the factory was a "safe place" for Christians, a place where they could talk openly about their faith. So the employees give the Nolans a great deal of credit even though the couple is not willing to accept that credit.

The company growth period (1998-present). With every part of the company now being bathed in prayer, both the business and the attendant ministries started taking off. The company was developing new products (some of them out of scrap materials from other products) and finding new markets for existing products. Jeff attributes this surge in creativity to having a close, personal relationship with "the most creative being in the universe." He gained confidence as an entrepreneur and innovator and became more selective about the work he was willing to accept. "In survival mode you will accept any work," he says. "In growth mode you look for better work."

As the company grew—sales were now in excess of one million dollars— the need for a stronger management team grew more acute. In response Jeff hired an American non-Christian man with extensive crosscultural management experience to be the production manager. The results, however, were disastrous. Specifically, the employees launched not one but *two* strikes in six months. The manager assured Jeff that there was nothing to worry about, that strikes were a regular occurrence in every factory he ever managed and that the problems always tended to get worked out. But Jeff was dumbstruck. He has always tried to run the company according to three basic principles: (1) people are more important than things, (2) relationships are more important than profits, and (3) eternal things are more important than temporal things. Clearly something had gone terribly wrong, and Jeff had little choice but to fire the manager.

Jeff learned an important lesson from this experience, and he is learning to be more sensitive to the subtle ways God brings the right people at the right time. This helps explain why, during a time when the need for a replacement production manager was becoming critical, he added a new member—Doug—whose principle business experience was working in microenterprise development for an international relief and development agency. Jeff and Doug had known each other for several years, and Jeff knew Doug was "a man after God's own heart." Thus when Doug started sharing his concern for a remote village six hours away, a place not only completely untouched by the gospel but also where the annual income was less than three hundred dollars, Jeff sensed God's quiet involvement and the opportunity his company had to bless this community in a variety of ways.

Over the next few months Jeff and Doug formulated a plan for a satellite factory that would become the production center for the simplest and least skill-intensive products (approximately 30 percent of the business). As Doug conducted the feasibility research for the new factory he visited a nearby village where he once worked and handpicked fourteen people who would be trained for leadership positions. During the six-week training period at the main factory, those people were also the focus of intense prayer coverage—five people from the ministry team prayed for *each* person *every* day. In the end, all fourteen made professions of faith, and based on his experience Jeff believes that probably half of those conversions were authentic. After the training they were sent back to their village along with a team of technical advisers, who not only oversaw the startup of the new factory but also continued the discipling process. Today the factory—with seventy employees—is the largest employer in the region. In addition to making urgently needed income, the community is also benefiting from improved health and hygiene and the expansion of other local businesses. Several churches are also now thriving in this formerly unreached village.

Company	Share of Sales
A	40%
B	35%
C	5%
D	5%
E	5%
Remaining customers	10%

Figure 7.1. Sales distribution by customer

All told, the two factories serve about 3 dozen customers, employ about 300 people and generate more than $2.2 million in revenues. As figure 7.1 shows, the company is still highly dependent on two customers, but Jeff has been taking some important steps toward diversifying the income stream. For example, he has hired a U.S.-based sales representative to expand sales of the most skill-intensive and profitable products, which attract an entirely new type of customer for the company. Currently these products comprise less than 10 percent of the business, but he hopes to see that figure grow to 40 percent within the next three years. He has set a revenue target of ten million dollars by 2006, and he anticipates that much of that growth will come from the new products. Two recent additions to the management team include a British-educated Nearstanian woman, who has been running factories for more than twenty years, and an American finance manager. All three new employees are kingdom professionals committed to the holistic mission of the company.

THE MINISTRY STORY

During the Nolans' first year in Farstan, two events occurred that laid the foundation for the ministry that would eventually grow out of the company. One was the arrest of an employee for nothing more than spending five minutes in prayer at work with Jeff and two other employees. The man—an active member of the Farstan church—was released without incident, but the episode quickly squelched any aspirations Jeff and Silvia might have had for a high-profile ministry in Farstan. Over the next few days Jeff brought his complaint before the Lord: "God, you brought me here, but now that I'm here, I can't say anything." The response he received was "So? Who said I wanted you to talk? I want you to *be* there, to *live* with them and *work* with them." Through this process the Nolans gained a better understanding of Bible passages such as Matthew 5:16: "Let your light shine before men, that they may see your good deeds and praise your Father in heaven."

The second building block was a Farstan man named Aaron, a committed Christian from a strong Christian family, who applied for a job at the company. Slow of mind but strong in body, Aaron was marked early in life as someone best suited for manual labor. By comparison, Aaron's brother was intelligent and articulate, and showed a strong potential for professional ministry. Aaron made a promise to his mother on her deathbed that he would provide for both his own family and his brother's, and thus enable his brother to pursue full-time ministry. It was within this context that he applied for a job at the Silk Road Handicraft Company. Jeff hired him and they soon began studying the Bible together. Aaron helped Jeff learn to read the Bible in the local language, and in the process Aaron learned how to not just read but also to *study* the Word.

Over time Jeff discovered that Aaron's slowness was more than offset by an unparalleled spiritual hunger and a passion for sharing God's love with others. Aaron soon began leading Bible studies of his own and ministering to his neighbors and coworkers. Still, no one fully appreciated the extent of his abilities and gifts until he was asked to look after his brother's ministries while his brother was out of the country attending seminary. Aaron accepted this responsibility and tended his brother's ministries in his usually diligent and faithful manner. When his brother returned four months later, the ministries had not only survived but also had *grown* under Aaron's leadership. Since then Aaron has been a respected part of the ministry leadership team, and almost every day of the week either a Bible study or a worship service takes place in his home.

At the factory Aaron's pastoral gifts and excellent people skills eventually earned him the title of human resources manager, a position that can resemble that of a pastor in many ways. As a regular part of his job, Aaron visits employees when they are sick or having problems at home. His job interviews have been known to last four hours or more. In these and other ways, his display of genuine concern for people not only reflects well on the company but also lays a solid foundation for long-term, trusting relationships. While a foreigner like Jeff naturally has trouble discerning the real needs from the exaggerated ones, Aaron is much more able to identify the truly needy. As a result, the company has been able to help numerous employees and their families by providing money for heart and eye operations, educational expenses and so forth.

Meanwhile Jeff and Silvia are now completely fluent in the language and are deeply involved in their own ministries of mercy, teaching and discipleship. The stories of individuals who have been shown the love of Christ through this couple in their home, in the village or in the factory could fill its own book. Yet probably the greatest privilege of all has been the opportunity they have had to work alongside—or more correctly, to work *under*—the local ministry leadership. "If there is already a church, you have no right to come in and meddle until you come under them and serve," Jeff says. "The role should be one of service to them. Whatever we do in terms of community outreach, we get permission first."

The local ministry leadership consists of almost two dozen men and women, many of them employees of the company, who are committed to seeing their village (about sixty thousand peopde) delivered from the spiritual forces that are oppressing it. The centerpiece of their strategy is prayer. On Thursday nights, for example, they meet for five hours of prayer focusing on the village, its government leaders and the people who would like to hinder their efforts. ("Five hours goes just like that.") On Saturdays they will often go "prayer walking" through the neighborhoods. The team also organizes a variety of outreach-oriented events for the local community. For example, on one recent weekend they rented four buses and brought about four hundred people to a local park for an evangelistic praise and worship service. Dozens accepted Christ that day. On another occasion they reserved a banquet room and threw a party, inviting only those who typically do not get invited to such things, like the poor, the crippled and the blind (see Lk 14:12-14). Their outreach to the local beggars is growing and has even spawned a church consisting entirely of former beggars.

PLANS FOR THE FUTURE

Jeff freely admits that he has not given the same attention to building the company's management team as he has to the ministry team: "We were so focused on finding people with the ministry skill sets that we needed that we neglected looking for people with the business skill sets." He now recognizes that as a business owner with hundreds of families dependent on the company, he has a moral responsibility to have qualified and experienced people at the management level. The recent additions certainly help, but there are still some significant weaknesses, particularly on the marketing side. To remedy this, Jeff is now working with other companies to create alliances that will strengthen this part of the business.

Assuming the company grows as he expects, he hopes to launch additional factories in other unreached parts of Farstan. His primary motivation for starting other satellite factories is to create opportunities to bring other resources to the community such as short-term teams of people who can treat the sick, teach and so on.

After months of prayer and fasting, the ministry team has embarked on an ambitious multiphase plan to reach not just their own village but also the surrounding city of 1.5 million people. The first phase was to move teams of three to four people into each of the village's six districts. These teams act as "lighthouses," praying for their neighbors, holding evangelistic Bible studies and so on.[2] Now that there is a team living in each district, they plan to start adding teams wherever they see God at work. God has confirmed in a number of ways that he is behind this plan, and they are now trusting him to draw twenty thousand people into new communities of faith over the next three years.

ANALYSIS AND CONCLUSIONS

Jeff is a highly exceptional case in many ways. He is seminary trained but chose to avoid the traditional missionary-sending-agency route. He launched a successful business even though he had little more than six months of actual business experience before coming to Farstan. He has a fairly traditional ministry background but does not view work as a distraction from ministry. As a general rule, people with his background tend to fail rather than succeed, and we do not recommend this for others with similar backgrounds. However, the story does illustrate several important points. First, there is no ironclad formula for success. We have found that, in his case as well as others, success seems to hinge more on one's relationship with God than on educational background or business acumen. Put another way, God can, and occasionally does, compensate for certain kinds of weaknesses. Second, this case is an excellent illustration of the freedom that comes with being an independent GCC. As a for-profit business accountable only to its shareholders, the company can be as involved in ministry as it wants to be. Blending business and ministry poses few if any legal problems.

In Jeff's case, however, independence also has arguably been the source of some of his problems. His case illustrates the value of having a group of people—a board—to help formulate strategy, coordinate the involvement of other stakeholders, recruit new team members and so on. Jeff is a creative, energetic person who never gives up. He typifies everything that is good about entrepreneurial people. However, like other highly innovative people, he also tends to lose interest in products once they become routine and simple to produce. Hence he has a tendency to develop new products rather than to aggressively compete against other firms. A good board can help remedy this by recruiting others to focus on the existing moneymaking products, thus freeing Jeff to do what he does best. (This is similar to what Microsoft did when it moved Bill Gates out of the CEO position and created for him the new position of chief software architect.)

We would be remiss if we concluded this chapter without pointing out the many things Jeff is doing well. In terms of ministry, he and Silvia assumed learners roles from the start, taking the time to learn the language and culture, and earning the right to speak to the locals about spiritual matters. Jeff submitted himself to the leadership of the indigenous church rather than asserting himself as the leader. In terms of the socioeconomic impact, 100 percent of the company's product is sold in export markets, and the profits are retained in the country. He links up with local firms and has even spun off a new factory in one of the neediest parts of the country. Jeff is also cultivating and equipping local leadership for both the business and its affiliated ministries. In other words, Jeff is doing everything right—partnering with and supporting the local church, and laying the groundwork for his own exit.

QUESTIONS FOR REVIEW

1. What were the important stages of Jeff Nolan's ministry preparation? His business preparation? In retrospect, what could he have done better?

2. What lessons can be learned from the early problems he experienced in Farstan?

3. If you were evaluating the Silk Road Handicraft Company according to the questions in the sidebar "Assessing the Viability of a GCC" (pp. 94-95), how would it measure up? What are its principle strengths and weaknesses?

4. We concluded that God can and does compensate for certain kinds of weaknesses. In what areas do you think God is less likely to compensate?

5. How can their strategy for reaching their village be applied to your own city?

8

THE INDEPENDENT, FACILITATIVE GCC

HOMESTEAD PARTNERS INTERNATIONAL

Supporting missionaries through private means (Lk 8:1-3)

ESTABLISHED: 1996

LOCATION: California

EMPLOYEES: eighteen

PROJECTED REVENUE (2003): $12 million

MISSION STATEMENT: To provide one-time and ongoing spiritual, emotional and physical support to missionaries and church organizations of like faith worldwide, and to provide opportunities for missionaries and laypeople of like faith to work in various trades related to acquiring, renovating and providing low- to moderate-income housing as a community ministry.

OVERVIEW

Homestead Partners International (HPI) is an innovative combination of nonprofit and for-profit organizations that was created for the express purpose of supporting, equipping and encouraging missionaries, with a primary emphasis on those working in the most neglected parts of the world. The ministry grew out of a simple prayer request—to be able to financially support some missionary friends—and has grown into an enterprise that has raised more than six million dollars for missions in six years. The money is raised not by donations, but through ordinary real estate transactions. In the process of supporting overseas missions, HPI is also servicing a wide variety of needs for the poor and homeless in California. According to the ministry's founder, "If a group of people with no business experience can do this, imagine what trained business men and women who are committed to advancing the kingdom can do." Today, with a highly skilled board and management team in place, HPI is investing in other Great Commission Companies and has set a goal of generating one hundred million dollars per year for missions by the year 2013. We classify HPI as an independent GCC because, while it works closely with established churches and mission organizations, it formulates its strategy much more independently than those labeled as alliances.

PERSONAL BACKGROUND

Craig Stewart (not his real name) had some exposure as a youth to the teachings of the Bible, but apart from his nominal Christian upbringing, he was not committed to any particular faith. He remembers watching *The 700 Club* from time to time, but mainly out of a curiosity based on the fact that Pat Robertson and his wife were regular customers of the Virginia Beach restaurant where he worked. Craig's impression of Robertson was favorable, partly because he was a generous tipper, one of those rare customers who would even tip the busboy. Craig's familiarity with Robertson would play an important role in his life several years later.

After high school Craig enlisted in the Air Force and began attending college at night. When his enlistment ended, he continued his schooling and eventually earned a degree in Criminal Justice, only to discover that he was not fond of working with criminals. Discouraged and struggling with questions about the direction and purpose of his life, Craig joined the Jehovah's Witnesses and moved to Florida, where he became an active door-to-door evangelist. One day he and his evangelism companion were having an earnest discussion with a pleasant, middle-aged Christian woman about, as always, the significance of the name Jehovah. Craig recalls: "Since she could not forcefully debate the significance or lack of significance of the name Jehovah, she simply tore out the page of her Bible wherein 'YHWH' was translated Jehovah, gave me the page, and said, 'Now you have what is important to you, the name Jehovah on this page; and I have what is important to me, Jesus Christ living in my heart.'"

This made an indelible impression on Craig. "I will never forget my thoughts. I knew she had something that was much more important and satisfying than what I had." The experience prompted him to quit the Jehovah's

Witnesses, reenlist in the Air Force and reenroll in college, this time with the goal of earning a master's degree in public administration. However, the stress of attending graduate school while working full time quickly began taking its toll, and his performance at work began to suffer. In traditional military fashion, his superiors responded by giving him the most difficult and unpleasant assignments, which caused his attitude and performance to deteriorate even further.

Craig was now thoroughly discouraged about the direction of his life. Nothing was working out the way he had planned, and any sense of fulfillment and purpose in life continued to elude him. This is when Robertson briefly reentered the picture. One morning at about five o'clock, after an especially tough and discouraging overnight shift, he returned to his barracks, slumped in front of the television, and thought, *My life is out of control.* At that very moment, the voice on the television asked, "Is your life out of control?" This immediately got his attention. It was Robertson explaining to the viewers that true happiness and purpose can only be found in Jesus Christ. Before he knew it he was on his knees in front of the television, asking Jesus to be his Lord and Savior.

Craig had no idea what to do next. He had no Christian friends and did not trust his own judgment, given his past experiences. So he prayed and asked God to send him someone who would help him learn more about the Christian faith. Not four hours later, that prayer was answered with a knock on the door. It was a man named Eric from an organization called The Navigators, and he wanted to know if Craig could spare a few minutes to talk about Christ. From that day forward Craig has never wavered in his belief that God answers prayer, and he never hesitates to bring everything before the Lord in prayer.

Not long after his conversion he met Lisa, a fellow noncommissioned officer, and the two quickly fell in love and decided to marry. Lisa claimed to be a Christian, and Craig had no reason to doubt that claim, but neither did he know enough to see that her assurance of salvation was based on a Christian heritage rather than on a personal relationship with Jesus. It was not until after their wedding that he realized she had no idea what it meant to be born again. This was a difficult way to begin a marriage, and things looked shaky at times, but after several years of persistent prayer on Craig's part, Lisa asked Jesus to be the Lord of her life.

When their military commitments were completed, they moved their two young children into a mobile home and enrolled in graduate school. Lisa decided to pursue a degree in school psychology, and Craig continued his work in pubic administration. On the side, they became involved in the ministry of Youth for Christ (YFC). Their home became a hub for youth ministry, sometimes with dozens of kids at a time hanging out or sleeping over. They loved working with youth and especially enjoyed seeing kids accept Christ and turn their lives around. It became obvious that this was their calling, and they decided to go into full-time ministry with YFC. Campus Life programs, which included weekly afterschool activities and spiritual and emotional nurture, were the core of their ministry in the local high schools. Many students were hearing about Jesus for the first time and accepting him as their personal Savior.

Probably no missionary likes raising financial support, but Craig and Lisa felt especially inept at this part of the job. Having both grown up outside evangelical Christianity, they lacked many of the advantages they felt other missionaries had, such as a preexisting network of potential supporters. As the family grew—now with five children—it became increasingly difficult to live on a mere seven hundred to one thousand dollars per month. They felt that something was fundamentally wrong with this approach to funding ministry. "There is nothing wrong with giving donations," says Craig. "God gave us his son; he is a giving God. He also asks us to be cheerful givers, and to tithe." But the idea that missionaries should be entirely dependent on donations is flawed. Perhaps it would work if Christians actually did tithe, speculates Craig, but given that the average Christian donates much less than 10 percent of his or her income, the church simply must find other ways to raise the necessary resources.

Eventually the Stewarts had little choice but to find part-time jobs to supplement their income—Craig as a substitute teacher and Lisa as a school psychologist. Until now they had never heard of bivocational missionaries or tentmakers, but they were soon going to discover the simplicity and the power of this approach. Specifically, their "secular" jobs allowed them to do something they were never able to do before: model their faith in front of others in a real-world setting. It is one thing to teach biblical principles in a small-group Bible study; it is quite another thing to teach those principles by modeling them every day on the job. Ministry was no longer something that was compartmentalized; it became integrated into their entire day. Having taken regular jobs, their relationships became richer, their witness more credible, their message more meaningful. Before the jobs, it was understood (or at least assumed) that the Stewarts were doing Campus Life work because that was what they were *paid* to do. The message the students received after the change was quite different; the Stewarts sincerely *cared* about them.

The school was so pleased with Craig's work that they asked him to teach full time. Recognizing this new direction as the will of God, they left YFC, and Craig returned to school for his teaching credential and began teaching high school English. They continued their ministry with Campus Life, but now as volunteers.

Craig was seeing kids accept Christ almost weekly. His passion for leading youth to Christ and seeing their lives turned around never wavered, and because of his unwillingness to keep Christ out of the classroom, he assumed that he would eventually be fired. "If you fully expect to get fired," he says, "the fear of getting fired loses its power." However, instead of getting him fired, his efforts earned him the unofficial title of campus chaplain. It also led to a new assignment: teaching the most difficult kids, those with chronic disciplinary problems and criminal records. Rather than seeing this as a punishment, Craig thrived in this environment because the school administrators gave him almost complete autonomy. The principal once told him, "I don't care what you do, so long as you keep them away from the other kids." What Craig "did" with the kids was pour his life into them. Without exception they all voluntarily attended the afterschool Campus Life meetings and became regular guests at the mobile home. Many committed their lives to Christ because of the incarnational ministries of Craig and Lisa.

The Stewarts' financial situation was now stable enough that they were able to buy a house. But they still had very little in the way of disposable income, and it grieved them that they were not able to give more money for missions. It reinforced their belief that "there has got to be a better way to fund missions." But exactly what, they did not know. One thing they did know was that God knows no limits and is merely looking for faithful stewards. They decided to make this a matter of daily prayer and in the process pledged that from this time forward they would give 51 percent of any new money that came into the household to missions. The sincerity of that prayer was almost immediately put to the test. For instance, within a few weeks they received an inheritance of ten thousand dollars from a relative they never knew. This was a large sum of money for a family of seven struggling to get by on school district salaries. Yet as promised they gave 51 percent to missions. A short time later they received an insurance settlement from a claim they never filed (but someone else filed anonymously on their behalf). Once again they followed through on their promise to give 51 percent of the money to missions. These were the tentative beginnings of a new ministry, a ministry of financial stewardship.

COMPANY HISTORY

Not long after the unexpected windfalls a friend presented the Stewarts with a novel fundraising idea: buy a house, renovate it and sell it for a profit. They knew that his motives were not entirely altruistic: he was, after all, a real estate agent. Nevertheless, the idea intrigued them, and they decided to borrow against the equity in their home and buy a fixer-upper. They spent nights and weekends renovating the house, then sold it for a net profit of ten thousand dollars. They promptly gave 51 percent to missions and used the balance to buy another house. The second experience did not go as smoothly, however, because a family emergency forced their work to a standstill. This put the family in a terrible bind. Barely able to afford one mortgage, it was never their intention to keep the second house for more than a couple of months.

Seeing their predicament, some friends from church decided to help finish the renovation. The house subsequently sold for a net profit of twelve thousand dollars. Their friends were so excited about the fundraising potential of this ministry that they asked the Stewarts to do it again. Craig and Lisa were understandably less eager, but they eventually agreed, and the third house was sold a couple of months later for another ten thousand dollars profit. The fun of this expensive, risky and time-consuming hobby was quickly wearing off, however, and they decided to quit after the third house. But then came an unpleasant surprise: capital gains taxes. Even though they had given away most of the proceeds, they were still facing a substantial tax liability. Thus they had little choice but to buy and renovate a fourth house to raise money for the tax.

By now, what began as a family fundraising "hobby" had grown into a loosely organized ministry involving about fifty people. Most were laypeople who were simply glad to have a new way to use their God-given skills for the kingdom. Others were missionaries on furlough who were helping in various ways in order to supplement their incomes. Soon the vision for HPI was born. Its mission: to provide "opportunities for missionaries and laymen of like faith to work in various trades . . . as a community ministry." More specifically it was to tap the abundant but underutilized resources of American churches and mobilize them for the sake of God's kingdom in less-developed and spiritually oppressed parts of the world.

HPI was incorporated as a religious nonprofit organization in March 1996. The first house the ministry bought turned out to be quite a story itself. As they removed drywall and pulled up flooring they discovered pentagrams and the carcasses of close to thirty animals that had been sacrificed in satanic rituals. A total of ninety-six cubic yards of filth had to be removed before they could start refurbishing the house. "We knew we were in the right place," recalls Craig. "We wanted to redeem this house." If that was not intimidating enough, a drive-by shooting took place in their front yard *while they were working on the house.* Sadly, in this neighborhood the shooting itself was only moderately newsworthy. What the local paper found to be more interesting was this strange group of people that was working on the house at the time of the shooting. Who were these people who wanted to buy run-down houses, work on them for free, and give away all the profits? The story, which ran the next day under the headline "Missionary Drive-by," attracted the attention of others in the housing industry. The experience also confirmed for the Stewarts that this ministry was about much more than simply raising money for missions: it was about helping families get a second chance in life and transforming neighborhoods that had long histories of crime, pain and satanic oppression.

The original management team and board of directors was an interesting mix of people. Most were past or present employees of the local school district: a tenth-grade teacher, a sixth-grade teacher and principal, and a school psychologist. Another was a former steel worker. What they brought to the table was an unwavering commitment to prayer and a distaste for the traditional donor-support approach to missions. What they lacked was any meaningful business experience. They knew that if this ministry was going to be financially sustainable, they had to learn something about business. What better place to start than the Bible? So they began meeting weekly as a group to study Larry Burkett's classic *Business by the Book*. For people who knew almost nothing about running a business, this was exciting stuff! Some of the principles they learned and decided to commit to include:

- *Pay your vendors promptly.* When a person does some work for the company, do not make him or her wait sixty days for payment. As tempting and common as this practice may be, Christians should be mindful of the fact that these people have families and expenses of their own. Thus the HPI board pledged to pay all bills not just quickly, but *immediately* upon receipt. They had no idea how they would fulfill that pledge, but they committed themselves to this principle and never regretted it. At times it was a close call, but somehow there has always been enough money to fulfill this commitment.

- *Put everything in writing.* If an agreement is not in writing, says Burkett, there is a 100 percent chance of a disagreement. This is especially important when Christians are working with or for other Christians because they all bring different notions of grace and stewardship.

- *Keep your promises.* From the very beginning HPI was determined to renovate every house as if Jesus himself were going to live there. Such a commitment was difficult and expensive to keep at times. They lost money on some houses as a result, sometimes lots of it, yet God always seemed to honor their faithfulness by giving them other opportunities that enabled them to recover those losses.

- *Get the right people for the job.* Just because someone is a Christian and is excited about your ministry does not mean he or she will be a good fit.

When hiring mistakes are made, everyone suffers. After firing almost thirty people—mostly missionaries—during the first two years, HPI has come to realize that character alone is no substitute for a professional skill set. A commitment to professionalism requires, well, professionals. It also requires a work ethic that, whether by nature or by nurture, seems to be lacking in many people who are accustomed to receiving donor support.

By implementing these principles, this ministry that was started by a ragtag group of educators has transformed into a highly professional team of real estate, construction, finance and social service professionals. The current board includes international business professionals and venture capitalists. Their reputation for integrity and professionalism began attracting the attention of a wide range of Christian professionals who wanted to redirect their energies. Rather than working hard and making some distant shareholders rich, they have joined HPI so those same skills can be used to generate income for God's work.

AFFORDABLE HOMES, RENTALS AND SHELTERS

Not long after the "Missionary Drive-by" story ran in the local paper, a mortgage professional approached them about participating in one of the federal government's affordable housing programs. In the program, approved non-profit providers of affordable housing can buy houses through this agency at discounted prices and favorable interest rates if they agree to renovate and sell the houses to low-income individuals and families. HPI researched the program, discussed it with the local agency director and decided to apply. Once approved, the agency allowed them to buy a couple of houses, and an inspector was sent to assess their work. Craig remembers telling the inspector about their commitment to renovate every house as if Jesus were moving in. The inspector was not sure what to make of that, but he had to admit that in his thirty-five years of inspecting houses for the government, he had never seen anything like these houses.

Their commitment to the "Jesus standard" was soon put to the test. In 1997 the agency approached them about a particularly unattractive house, one that could not possibly be refurbished to a "Jesus standard" without the loss of a substantial amount of money. Craig suspects the agency was testing them. Would they stick to their commitment even if it meant losing money? HPI bought the house, renovated it and subsequently lost forty-four thousand dollars. The agency was so appreciative (no other nonprofit organization would take it) they followed up by offering three more houses that needed little more than minor cosmetic work. HPI made eighty thousand dollars on those three houses, and by 1998 it was named the agency's "Non-Profit of the Year" for that part of the state.

Craig believes HPI's "Joseph mentality" is a big reason for its success. "We want to do what we can to make Pharaoh look good, because ultimately God is going to use Pharaoh to bless his people." Soon they were presented with another opportunity to bless Pharaoh. They discovered another government program for nonprofits that provides affordable rental housing for the poor and homeless, with priority given to homeless veterans and their families. HPI saw several opportunities with this program. First, the ability to buy—and keep—deeply discounted homes enabled them to significantly improve their balance sheet and increase their borrowing capacity. Second, the program comes with an obligation to regularly minister to these families for a minimum of three years. The services the government requires them to provide include connecting the tenants to public and private providers of financial counseling, Aid to Families with Dependent Children, Section 8 housing assistance and so on. Informally it also enabled HPI to develop meaningful long-term relationships with the families. Their experience and unwavering commitment to quality helped them receive approval for this program, and HPI is now one of the largest providers of affordable housing in the state of California.

Table 8.1 summarizes the first seven years of HPI's home-buying activity. It is worth noting two problems they have had along the way. First, the rental-housing program is highly sensitive to economic cycles. Homes are only made available to nonprofits if they remain unsold on the open market for ninety days. Thus in 1997 and 1998 HPI bought thirty-six such homes, but since then no homes have remained on the market long enough for them to buy. The majority of the activity throughout HPI's history has been with the first government agency, along with a smattering of homes that were purchased on the open market with no strings attached.

Table 8.1. HPI's Home-Buying Activities

Year	Number of Homes	Total Revenue	Net Profit	Donated to Missions
1996	2	n.a.	n.a.	n.a.
1997	61	$724,680	$336,276	$227,045
1998	63	$1.31 million (not audited)	$683,877	$419,556
1999	62	$5.91 million	$418,837	$237,896
2000	111	$10.26 million	$797,741	$337,081
2001	99	$9.9 million	$541,452	$364,825
2002	19	$7.35 million	$1,252,063	$376,442 (plus $301,500 invested in GCCs)
2003 (projected)	75	$9.4 million	$937,500	$478,000
2004 (projected)	120	$15 million	$1.5 million	$765,000

In 2000, HPI bought 111 homes from this agency, and in 2001 another 99. However, when the agency began to see the enormous amounts of money that were being made, alarm bells went off and the entire program was suspended. All nonprofits were forced to reapply. In the intervening six months, almost everything else HPI was doing came to a standstill. An estimated $12.5 million in revenue was lost, not to mention the enormous amount of time and energy that went into refiling under the newer, more restrictive rules. Today there is a cap on the number of houses a nonprofit may purchase (determined on a case-by-case basis) as well as on the amount of profit that can be earned from each house. HPI was finally reapproved in early 2002, but a seventy-five-home annual limit is now in place. On the bright side, in early 2003 HPI received statewide approval, and they expect their integrity and superior performance will eventually result in approvals in other states as well as an increased limit to the number of houses they can buy in each state.

THE HOMESTEAD MORTGAGE GROUP

In the process of buying, renovating, and selling or renting so many houses, HPI spends a great deal of money every year on things like landscaping, residential cleaning services, termite inspection and fumigation, and mortgage brokerage fees. The ideal situation would be to own some of these businesses as a way to both control costs and diversify the ministry's income stream. However, there are legal limits to how much "unrelated business income"—meaning income from corporately owned assets that are not part of the organization's core mission—nonprofits can receive. So instead, HPI created the Homestead Mortgage Group (HMG), a wholly owned, for-profit subsidiary that donates 100 percent of its net profit to missions. Because HPI receives no income from HMG, and there are no outside shareholders who can benefit inappropriately from HPI's business, this structure minimizes the risk of any conflicts of interest that would threaten their tax-exempt status.

Their mortgage brokerage, Homestead Mortgage Services (HMS), has been especially successful. Like the other companies, HMS not only services the needs of HPI but also competes very successfully in the open market. The company, which is headed by a kingdom professional woman with substantial industry experience, specializes in offering loan services and pre-qualification assistance to first-time homebuyers and guiding them through the home financing process. Often these services are provided in conjunction with free seminars that are offered in churches and community centers statewide.

PROJECT REFERRAL

Because real estate commissions are a significant expense for HPI, one of the businesses it formed inside the Homestead Mortgage Group was a real estate brokerage. As a licensed broker, HMG can participate in one of the industry's most basic, customary practices—referrals—and, more important, can collect referral fees whenever they refer a buyer or seller to another broker. If the referral results in a sale, a referral fee of 25 percent of the selling broker's commission is customarily paid to the referring broker. The income can be substantial for something as simple as connecting someone to a qualified broker. For example, on a house that sells for $267,000, the standard referral fee would be a little over $2,000.

The entrepreneurial question then becomes, how can you generate a *stream* of referrals and make a business out of it? The answer: advertise on Christian radio and give listeners an incentive to use HMG's referral system. The incentive? Donate the entire referral fee to missions and ministries, and allow the listener to designate where half of it goes. Specifically, 10 percent is automatically earmarked for the listener's home church, another 15 percent for the local chapter of Youth for Christ (thanks to the ties that bind the Stewarts to YFC), and 25 percent goes to fund overseas missions of HMG's

HOW THE REFERRAL PROGRAM WORKS

Suppose a house sells for $200,000. The seller's broker receives a 3 percent commission, or $6,000. HMG receives a 25 percent fee for the referral, or $1,500.

To determine how that money is distributed, follow these steps:

Step 1:	Multiply referral fee by 50%	$750 (for the ministry or missionary of choice)
Step 2:	Multiply referral fee by 10%	$150 (for local church)
Step 3:	Multiply referral fee by 15%	$225 (for the local chapter of Youth for Christ)
Step 4:	Multiply referral fee by 25%	$375 (for overseas missions of HMG's choice)

Notice that without any additional cost to the buyer or seller, $1,500 has been generated for ministries and missionaries.

Significant dollars for significant ministry!

choice. (If the buyer does not attend a Christian church, 10 percent is donated to The National Center for Fathering.) The remaining 50 percent goes
to the nonprofit organization of the listener's choosing. HMG staff follows
the escrow process and ensures that the fees are distributed correctly. By going through HMG, the customer loses nothing, as this money would have
been paid anyway, and gains the satisfaction of knowing that part of the
commissions were used to bless a variety of ministries.

The company estimates that if it can capture just half a percent of the real
estate transactions in California alone, over one billion dollars per year would
be raised for ministry. If expanded nationwide, this single business idea has
the potential of generating as much income for missions and ministries as all
other income sources combined. Unfortunately, the program has been tem-
porarily halted until God brings the right person along who can build this
into a national program and give this effort the necessary leadership.

THE MINISTRY STORY

Clearly it is impossible to make a precise distinction between the business
and ministry of Homestead Partners. In the course of generating income for
its ministry of supporting, equipping and encouraging missionaries, it is
making home ownership a reality for low-income families and providing affordable housing and other services to the poor and homeless. Furthermore,
in the course of helping meet people's housing needs, it is working in partnership with churches and other local ministries to meet other physical,
emotional and spiritual needs. Recognizing that everything this nonprofit
and its network of for-profit companies does is for a charitable purpose, we
will focus our attention on the way it uses its *surplus* income. Indeed the fact
that this ministry is not only self-sufficient but also generates surplus income is truly extraordinary. In six years it has generated more than six million dollars in net income and donated or invested more than three million
in ministries in less-developed or less-reached countries. In this section we
will highlight just a few of the things they are doing with that money.

In the early days they were thrilled simply to be able to support any overseas missionary or ministry. All told, they directly supported almost three
dozen missionaries, some at levels of one thousand dollars per month, and

helped fund things like equipment purchases for medical clinics. However, they "quickly learned that it is very easy to create a dependency cycle," Craig recalls. Their efforts have more recently been directed toward helping ministries break the cycle of dependency by helping them start—and usually by giving them—viable, income-producing businesses. This is part of a broader strategy to help build the infrastructure upon which front-line missionaries and agencies rely. Craig is fond of reminding people that the reason Hitler's Germany lost its war against Russia was because he overextended himself, pushing his army too far ahead of its supply lines. In a similar way, Craig believes, the efforts of mission agencies suffer from a poorly supported infrastructure. Income generation, technological support and transportation are just a few of the infrastructure-related areas HPI is attempting to strengthen.

One area of disappointment, however, has been in helping ministries become less donor-dependent. In 2001 they began pursuing a strategy that involved in some cases setting up dedicated HMS franchises within other ministries, and in other cases equipping and training ministries to run their own home-refurbishing programs. The ownership and operation of these businesses would reside with the individual ministries, and the income would be used to support their operations budget. After some initial expressions of interest and initial successes by some fairly high-profile ministries and mission organizations, Craig was convinced he was witnessing the beginnings of a paradigm shift in the way evangelically oriented nonprofits funded their operations. Less would have to come out of the missionaries' financial support and more would be generated through businesses.

By 2003, however, that optimism was gone. In every single case where HPI equipped and trained the ministry—at significant cost to itself—the businesses that were started are now defunct. Whenever a problem was encountered, like the loss of a key person who was running the business, the leaders of the nonprofit lost interest and returned instead to seeking handouts from HPI. Craig now believes that there is something about the traditional "ministry mentality" that is stubbornly unwilling to be involved with running a business: "Most organizations just see us as a cash cow and are not interested in doing business as missions themselves." He is still open to the idea of helping ministries in this way, but is determined to be much more selective in the future.

Partly as a consequence of this strategy's failure to bear fruit, HPI is now pursuing a slightly different strategy that is still consistent with its core mission of supporting, equipping and encouraging missionaries. It includes things like buying property on which orphanages can grow, buying equity stakes in GCCs and funding micro-loan projects, all with the aim of facilitating the spread of the gospel in the less-developed and less-reached parts of the world. All told, they have invested more than six hundred thousand dollars in projects of this nature. In addition, they continue to give one-time gifts toward worthy causes like family camps, orphanages, missionary retreat centers and direct church-planting efforts both at home and abroad.

PLANS FOR THE FUTURE

Despite recent restrictions imposed by the federal government, HPI has set an ambitious goal of generating $100 million annually for missions within ten years. It has outlined a four-pronged strategy for achieving that goal. First, it will apply for approvals in other states to operate as a federal low-income housing provider, thus increasing the minimum number of houses it can buy and sell each year. Second, once a suitable kingdom professional is in place, they hope to re-launch the mortgage referral program, this time nationwide. The third prong involves continuing its efforts to form alliances with like-minded nonprofits that are interested in integrating business into their ministries. And finally, probably the most ambitious prong involves the recent hiring of a Christian man with extensive experience in the banking and savings and loan (S&L) industries, including experience with turning failing banks around, and the purchase of a savings and loan institution (in the final stages of negotiation as of April 2003).

Unlike banks, S&Ls are required by law to keep most of their money in real estate loans. For most people this restriction makes S&Ls less attractive investments than banks, but for a nonprofit affordable housing provider and mortgage broker it offers many attractive possibilities. As federally regulated financial institutions, S&Ls have access to the lowest possible interest rates. Craig estimates that their own mortgage transactions alone would be enough for the S&L to nearly break even. If they can win even a fraction of the mortgage business of other nonprofit affordable housing providers—

there are currently 672 nonprofit affordable housing providers in the United States that process some nine thousand transactions each year—the income potential is staggering. Because access to capital is one of the choke points in the affordable housing market, they are confident that by focusing on the needs of the nonprofit housing provider, they can get a substantial share of that business. In addition, they plan to offer other services through the S&L to the nonprofit sector, such as assistance with real estate purchases, filing requirements and regulatory compliance.

Their experience as investors in GCCs elsewhere in the world also has led HPI to start thinking more creatively about ways they can use other businesses and networks of businesses to the benefit of people in less-developed countries. Few specifics can be discussed here, but HPI's track record thus far gives us confidence that many of those efforts will be successful. A key part of that strategy involves relying on mission agencies and local churches to provide the human resources, while HPI supports the infrastructure and additional resources such as technology support, real estate management and more.

EVALUATION AND CONCLUSIONS

What began as a humble, volunteer-led effort has grown into a finely tuned, highly professional enterprise. HPI is another illustration of a familiar trend: Christians who believe in the Great Commission's contemporary relevance become active in ministry and eventually start reaching beyond their own people group. After assessing their resources—time, skills and money—they set out to use those resources in the most strategic and efficient way. The Stewarts were humble enough to recognize the need to commit this completely to God's leadership and to rely on God's Word for their basic business principles. "The technical skills of operating a business can be fairly easily learned," says Craig. "But if you don't know who you're serving in your business, you will end up serving the business." By committing themselves to prayer and to following biblical business principles, HPI has been growing "in wisdom and stature, and in favor with God and men" (Lk 2:52). They also recognize the importance of having a well-qualified management team and board of directors, and have strengthened these areas considerably since they first began. During one transitional period Craig was both CEO and chairman of the board, but that was out of necessity, not by choice. The current chairman is a kingdom professional with extensive experience in mergers, acquisitions and investing in "social ventures"—for-profit companies that have a social agenda (some Christian, but not all).

Some may see the company's ten-year goal of giving one hundred million dollars annually to missions as farfetched, given its current size and capabilities. However, from what we know about the management team and its commitment to faith, prayer and professionalism, the skeptics would be well advised to take that figure seriously. Even if they reach only half of their goal, this company-ministry will have nearly matched the entire frontier missions giving of the church. Imagine what can happen if an entire generation of Christian business professionals follows suit by committing their energies and talents to the cause of Christ.

QUESTIONS FOR REVIEW

1. What were the important stages of the Stewarts' ministry preparation? Their business preparation? Given where they are now, what could they have done better to prepare?

2. Do you agree with Craig that those who have a traditional "ministry mentality" are stubbornly unwilling to change the way they finance their ministries? If so, do you believe this is a permanent condition or one that can change? Why?

3. If you were evaluating HPI according to the questions in the sidebar "Assessing the Viability of a GCC" (pp. 94-95), how would it measure up? What are its principle strengths and weaknesses?

4. Use your imagination to come up with another business that could be integrated into a nonprofit ministry.

9
THE FACILITATIVE ALLIANCE

PURA VIDA COFFEE
Great Coffee, Great Cause™

ESTABLISHED: 1998

LOCATION: Seattle, Washington

EMPLOYEES: Sixteen in United States, six in Costa Rica and six independent
          sales agents

PROJECTED REVENUE (2003): $1.8 million

MISSION STATEMENT: To build a profitable company that generates a
sustainable source of funding for Christian ministry, provides a meaningful, faith-
centered workplace for employees and reflects the character and love of Jesus.

OVERVIEW
Pura Vida Coffee, LLC, sells branded, fresh-roasted coffee through direct
channels such as the Internet and toll-free order lines, as well as indirectly
through church fundraisers and strategic partnerships with established
charitable organizations such as World Relief and Habitat for Humanity. This
young, fast-growing company was founded in 1998 by two former business
school classmates—John Sage and Chris Dearnley—expressly for the purpose of being the "funding engine" for Christian ministries that are helping
meet the physical, emotional and spiritual needs of at-risk children in Costa
Rica and other coffee-growing countries. The company is a subsidiary of
Pura Vida Partners, a tax-exempt, nonprofit corporation that oversees those
outreach programs. In accordance with its bylaws and charter, the company
donates 100 percent of its net profit to Pura Vida Partners and other ministries that are not only providing these kids with hot meals, clothing and

medical care but also sharing the gospel and helping build self-esteem. Pura Vida Partners also accepts donations from individuals and corporations. The company's philanthropic focus is a key source of competitive advantage. Yet the company does not expect its customers to buy only because of the charitable purpose. "We compete on our merits," says John. "We don't ask customers to make any tradeoffs in terms of quality or service, and we don't ask them to pay an above-market price. We compete on our merits, then we share the stories of the kids whose lives are being changed through this ministry." The company's commitment to give away all of its net profit has created some interesting problems as well, specifically in terms of its ability to raise additional capital. Its solution to this problem is itself an important financial innovation and a potential model for other Great Commission Companies.

PERSONAL BACKGROUND
John Sage. The Pura Vida story begins with two people from vastly different backgrounds. John Sage grew up in Berkeley, California, during the 1960s and 1970s in a family that was, as John mildly puts it, "socially active." His parents were squarely middle-class folks—Dad worked for the federal government and Mom was a school teacher—but they were also deeply involved in the anti-war protests and social activism that Berkeley is known for. At age eleven John saw nothing unusual about the fact that he was walking precincts in support of George McGovern's presidential campaign. Nor did he see the occasional encounters with riot police and tear gas—with his family—as particularly out of the ordinary childhood experience. His family belonged to a church that was deeply involved in the same social causes but, as John recalls, treated Christianity as a cerebral, academic concept, not as something involving an actual, personal relationship with a living Lord.

His parents were also alcoholics in the "two cocktails or a bottle of wine every night" sense. It was not uncommon for his parents to return home drunk at night, which left it up to John to not only take care of his younger brother but also his inebriated parents. Not surprisingly, John grew up fast and developed a strong sense of self-reliance that has both helped and hindered him in different ways ever since.

John left for Stanford University after high school to begin pursuing a degree in American Studies. He quickly discovered, however, that good grades would require more study time than his work schedule allowed. If he was going to do well in school, he simply had to find a way to earn more than minimum wage. His solution? Start a business. The first business was a birthday cake delivery service, which targeted freshman parents with banners on the first day of class that read, "Remember your kids on their birthday!" John and his business partner would accept the orders and the payments for literally thousands of birthday cakes, then negotiate with local bakeries for the best price. After that it was simply a matter of delivering the cakes on the appropriate dates. They did not get particularly rich with that business, but as John recalls, "It was a great way to meet freshman girls."

Some people are naturally gifted at seeing opportunities where others do not. John's second business idea is another example. Campuses are full of bicycles. Most people see them merely as a low-cost form of transportation. But John saw something much more; he saw two-wheeled, mobile billboards. He designed a triangular fiberglass billboard that could be mounted to the frame of a bicycle, and he went to work selling advertising space to local merchants, paying students twenty-five dollars per month for the use of their bikes. This company, which was aptly named Bike Boards, proved to be even more successful than the first. He would eventually expand the company across a dozen campuses. Together these two forays into the world of business start-ups revealed a gift for entrepreneurship, and it planted a seed within him to one day combine his passions for business and social justice.

After graduating in 1983 John accepted a job as a lobbyist for a large pharmaceutical company. As a single, straight male in San Francisco who was making good money, John felt like he had it all. At least that is what he thought until one night when he had a strange dream, one that he can hardly describe except to say that he "felt the presence of the Lord." The experience left him with such a profound sense of joy that all he could do was weep. A few days later, an old acquaintance invited him to attend a luncheon organized by the Christian Business Men's Committee (CBMC, now called Connecting Business Men to Christ). John, who rarely was free for lunch, had a last-minute cancellation that day and agreed to attend. It was there that he heard for the first time a man describing his faith as something alive and personal, not abstract and intellectual like all the other "Christians" John had known. The man's testimony, combined with the warmth and joy John still remembered from his "dream," prompted him to commit his life to Christ that afternoon. Later that day he bought a Bible and began reading it. He had read parts of the Bible before, "but never with the expectation of meeting Jesus."

The following year was a year of spiritual growth and discipleship (mainly through CBMC's Operation Timothy). During that year he also decided to quit the pharmaceutical company and, after a brief stint with a revived and expanded Bike Boards, enrolled in Harvard University's MBA program.

Chris Dearnley. Chris was born and raised outside Philadelphia. His exposure to the gospel began when he was about five years old, when his parents both turned the controls of their lives over to Jesus. He eventually accepted Christ himself, but describes it as more of an intellectual faith, not one that was particularly personal or powerful. Still, he grew up in an evangelical, missions-minded family and participated in a wide variety of short-term missions trips, including trips to Haiti, Jamaica and Venezuela, where he was able to see God working in circumstances that were far different from his own upper-middle-class American experience.

His relationship with Jesus took an important turn when, as a sophomore at Wheaton College, he participated in a summer-long youth hostel ministry in Amsterdam's red-light district. For the first time he saw the reality and power of evil and the oppression that inevitably goes along with occultism. He also saw the amazing countervailing power of the gospel and the ability it has to deliver people from the oppression of the evil one. He realized that "truth and power need to be combined," and began crying out in his soul, "God, I believe, but why am I not experiencing this power?" From that day forward Chris has been experiencing the joy and the power that only Jesus can provide.

His remaining three years at Wheaton were a time of tremendous growth. Chris participated in other ministries and missions trips, and even attended Penn State for two separate terms as a way of strengthening his faith. After graduating from Wheaton with a degree in economics, he led a team of students on a missions trip to Bolivia, then moved to Costa Rica to attend language school. His plan was to stay for only six months, but he ultimately accepted a job with an economic and business development organization called Opportunity International (OI). In addition to working for them, he was involved in other ministries and ultimately helped plant a church. After leaving OI he worked independently as a consultant, then later for a Costa Rican exporting company. He spent six years in Costa Rica before he felt it was time to move on. Business school sounded like a logical next step, so he applied and was accepted to Harvard's MBA program.

Kindred spirits. John and Chris both entered Harvard in the fall of 1987. John had been out of school for four years and Chris for six. The challenge of returning to school after many years was a bit intimidating, and they each eagerly accepted an invitation to attend a get-together organized by the Harvard chapter of InterVarsity's Graduate Student Fellowship. This is where the two first met and immediately became friends. Among other things, they began meeting every morning for prayer and coffee before class. John recalls that those prayers often amounted to little more than entreaties for God's help to make it through the first year. "It didn't always look like we would make it," he remembers with a lingering tinge of relief. Their prayers were answered, and they graduated in the spring of 1989.

After graduation they embarked on two very different careers. Chris, now married to a woman who was as sincere as he about being used by God, moved back to Costa Rica and directed the Coalition of Christian Colleges and Universities' study-abroad program there. Because they were newly married, however, the couple decided to return to the States a year later, and he began working for a company that helped executives from Fortune 500 companies prepare for life in Latin America.

The desire to do something more significant for Costa Rica never left, however, and in 1995 they decided to return to that country, this time as church planters with the Vineyard. Before long Chris was pastoring a growing church in an upper-middle-class neighborhood in San Jose, Costa Rica. Soon after the church started, God impressed on Chris an image of a bridge, which Chris understood to mean that his church was to serve as a bridge, not only across cultures but also across classes and denominations. Thus when a pastor from a tough, drug-infested neighborhood in another part of town came to the church and shared about the work his church was doing to reach the kids there, Chris seized the opportunity. The man's challenge was "Help me reach the kids in this neighborhood because they are the addicts of the future." The following week, a group of volunteers from Chris's church mustered the courage to drive to the crime-plagued neighborhood and began ministering in whatever way they could. Chris admits that at the time "we had no idea what we were doing." They handed out hot dogs, played with the children, told Bible stories and basically considered each trip a success if no fights broke out. "We were happy if there was no blood on the pavement at the end of the day," Chris recalls.

Meanwhile John was indulging his passion for the fast-paced world of business startups. His first job after Harvard was with a relatively young company called Microsoft, where he worked as a senior manager for its Applications Division and later directed the marketing and launch of the company's newly developed flagship product, Microsoft Office. His five years with the company were fascinating, even "intoxicating," but the hundred-hour workweeks were taking their toll. The fifth year was particularly stressful because, in addition to the launch of MS Office, he married Shelly, a friend from Stanford, and his younger brother died from AIDS-related complications. Emotionally and spiritually drained, John decided to leave Microsoft and take some time off to rest and to reevaluate where he was going with his life. Once again his thoughts turned toward finding a way to use his gifts for some higher purpose.

As is often the case when people wish for greater spiritual significance, John began considering following in the footsteps of his good friend Chris by going into full-time ministry. He even began filling out an application for seminary before realizing that he had "no interest whatsoever in seminary." Instead, and in the absence of any better ideas, he joined the marketing and executive team for a new startup called Starwave Corporation, a company started by Microsoft cofounder Paul Allen that developed entertainment websites for organizations like the National Basketball Association, National Football League and ESPN. John enjoyed the work immensely, but when Disney acquired Starwave three years later, it left him wealthy but once again wondering how he could integrate his passions for business and ministry.

John describes himself as being "long on cash but short on vision" during this period. However, that began to change when, as a board member for the Northwest AIDS Foundation, he was put in charge of finding ways to solidify the foundation's funding base. One idea he came up with was a gift basket—the Red Ribbon Sampler, they eventually called it—that contained a Starbucks coffee sampler and a classical CD. They marketed the thirty-dollar gift baskets primarily to corporations that appreciated not only the gift's distinctiveness but also the fact that for every basket purchased, eight dollars went directly to a good cause. In the process of working on this project, John caught the attention of the Starbucks Corporation, who then hired him as a consultant to help develop ways to fund their own charitable foundation. Once again John thrived in this environment and came up with several groundbreaking ideas. But more important, it gave him an inside look at the coffee industry and helped him see how a good product can be combined with a good cause for mutual benefit.

THE BIRTH OF A GREAT COMMISSION COMPANY

Over the years Chris and John stayed in close contact, meeting at least once a year to catch up with and encourage each other. It was during one of those annual get-togethers in 1997 that John, along with another friend from Harvard named Kent Coykendall, listened to Chris's stories about lives being transformed in Costa Rica with what John describes as "a strange mixture of feelings." What this small group of people was doing with their meager resources was truly amazing and inspiring. By working in partnership with other ministries, Chris's church was now reaching the community through a soup kitchen, a computer training and job placement center, a drug rehabilitation center and a kids club. A new church was also now thriving in this community. Chris shared what seemed like countless stories of people's lives being turned around and of kids being turned away from drugs and crime toward lives as productive, law-abiding citizens. The biggest challenge at this point was money. Much of the funding came from an inheritance Chris had received eight years earlier that was now almost gone.

While the three friends brainstormed about possible funding solutions,

John shared about his experiences with Starbucks. Then, almost as an after-thought, Chris reached into his bag and tossed John and Kent a bag of coffee he had brought from Costa Rica. Instead of the expected thank-you, John's first reply was "How much did this cost?" Within seconds the trio was work-ing on a business plan for a company that would sell gourmet coffee to indi-viduals over the Internet and to churches and ministries, and would donate 100 percent of its net profits to ministries in coffee-growing countries around the world. Kent brought a strong operations background to the discussion, John brought extensive marketing experience, and Chris "coincidentally" knew a lot about the production and sourcing side of the business. Together they spent the next four to five hours fleshing out the idea. John would sup-ply the start-up capital and run the company from an office in Seattle, and Chris would work with the coffee suppliers in Costa Rica. Before the meeting ended, however, Chris made one last recommendation, an unusual one, at least for John and Kent. He suggested they do nothing but pray for the next month. He correctly pointed out that if this venture was something God wanted them to pursue, one month would not make any difference. On the other hand, if it was *not* God's desire, then that month of prayer would have saved them "a lot of pain." Of course John is not the type of person who can sit still for long when he is chomping at the bit of a new idea. But he recog-nized the unnaturalness of this act and did, after all, want to build a prayer-centered company. Thankfully they received "abundant confirmation," as John says, during that month that God was supportive of this plan.

THE COMPANY STORY

Pura Vida Coffee was officially launched in August 1998 as a limited liability company (LLC). The company name was Chris's idea. Literally translated it means "pure life," but the term is more broadly used in Costa Rica as a greet-ing or an expression of encouragement like "awesome," "way to go" or "cool." At first the company took care of all the sourcing and distribution it-self. But it quickly became apparent that sourcing and roasting the coffee in Costa Rica was not the best way to grow this business. In addition to limiting the range of products they could offer, the business model required the com-pany to anticipate potentially wide swings in demand and maintain large inventories of coffee. Given that freshness is one of the most important product qualities in the specialty coffee market, holding large inventories simply was not acceptable. John solved these problems by forming alliances with several companies, including coffee importers in Seattle and Atlanta (Atlas Coffee and Cooperative Coffees) and roasters in each city (Dillanos and Partners Coffee). These relationships enabled Pura Vida to expand its product line to include coffees from other countries, including organic, "fair trade" and shade-grown coffees, and they allow the company to fill orders on demand. These alliances also enable the company to handle unexpectedly large orders and fluctuating seasonal demands very efficiently.

CUSTOMERS

Pura Vida's promise of "Great Coffee, Great Cause™" resonates especially well among faith-based and socially conscious consumers of coffee.[1] It engenders intense brand loyalty and unprompted word-of-mouth recommendations. The company classifies those customers into three main groups:

- *Commercial customers.* These include high-volume buyers (one thousand or more pounds per year) such as colleges and universities (Portland State, Azusa Pacific, Point Loma, Evergreen State and many others) and institutional food service providers. Commercial customers typically sign multi-year contracts, agree to purchase a minimum of twenty pounds of coffee per month and provide exposure for the company's products to prospective individual customers. Pura Vida's service to these customers also includes items such as cups, filters and brewing equipment.

- *Personal customers.* These are individuals who purchase directly from the website (<www.puravidacoffee.com>) or call the toll-free order line (877-469-1431). In the process many choose to join Pura Vida's monthly subscription program, Constant Cup, as well as add a charitable donation to their orders, which is passed on directly to Pura Vida Partners. By early 2003, more than $192,000 in small donations had been collected this way.

- *Partners.* These are organizations such as Habitat for Humanity, World Relief, Episcopal Relief and Development and Sojourners that buy "partner" or cobranded coffee in bulk quantities (for example, Habitat for Humanity's "House Blend"). The coffee is then utilized either for institutional use or for fundraisers whereby their constituents (donors, supporters, volunteers and so forth) are encouraged to buy the product as a means of supporting the organization's particular work.

Given the company's philanthropic purpose, a central part of the marketing strategy is to target customers who will be attracted by the company's socially responsible products and purpose. Pura Vida does not focus exclusively on Christians, but John says focusing on Christians nevertheless makes good sense, given there are an estimated fifty million Christian coffee drinkers in the United States alone.

FINANCIAL RESULTS AND GROWTH STRATEGY

Since its inception Pura Vida has demonstrated consistent and dramatic sales growth, with annual increases of 153 percent in 2001 and 115 percent in 2002. The company nearly reached the one-million-dollar mark in sales for 2002 and is expecting to double its sales once again in 2003. Moreover, its gross margins are improving as a result of its ability to control operating expenses (as a percent of sales, these are declining) and to create synergistic relationships with experienced partners. The bulk of the infrastructure investment and capital expenditures were made in 2000 and 2001, investments that the company predicts will result in sustained profitability by the fourth quarter of 2004. Before-tax earnings (EBT) are expected to exceed $2.4 million by 2010.

The company's ambitious growth strategy includes the following:

- Add at least eighty new commercial accounts in 2003 and accelerate that pace in subsequent years while also retaining at least 90 percent of existing accounts.

- Leverage its relationships with Christian bookstore chains by providing them with attractive and high-return displays that generate brand awareness and retail sales.

- Launch new partnerships with a select group of national ministries, including the recently completed partnership with Episcopal Relief and Development.

Table 9.1. Financial Summary

$'000	1999 Actual	2000 Actual	2001 Actual	2002 Actual	2003 Forecast	2004 Forecast	2005 Forecast	2006 Forecast	2010 Forecast
				Year ended/ending December 31,					
Sales	$ 34	$ 151	$ 382	$ 821	$ 1,799	$ 2,916	$ 4,026	$ 5,268	$ 11,009
Gross Margins	(35)	34	127	318	708	1,162	1,645	2,176	4,892
Sales & Marketing	29	104	476	490	546	615	693	814	1,299
Technology & Administration	87	286	414	445	449	531	587	691	1,083
EBITDA	(151)	(356)	(763)	(617)	(287)	16	365	671	2,510
Other Income/(Expense)	-	-	(38)	(88)	(169)	(188)	(196)	(160)	(49)
EBT	$ (151)	$ (356)	$ (801)	$ (705)	$ (456)	$ (172)	$ 169	$ 511	$ 2,461
Revenue Growth % yr on yr	nr	344.1%	153.0%	114.9%	119.1%	62.1%	38.1%	30.8%	27.2%
Gross Margin %	nr	22.5%	33.2%	38.7%	39.4%	39.8%	40.9%	41.3%	44.4%
EBT Margin %	nr	-235.8%	-209.7%	-85.9%	-25.3%	-5.9%	4.2%	9.7%	22.4%
Expense as % of Sales									
- Sales & Marketing	85.3%	68.9%	124.6%	59.7%	30.4%	21.1%	17.2%	15.5%	11.8%
- Technology & Administration	255.9%	189.4%	108.4%	54.2%	25.0%	18.2%	14.6%	13.1%	9.8%

nr - ratio analysis limited due to the start up nature of the operations. Infrastructure developed in 1999/2000 with sales development commencing 2001.

- Significantly expand personal retail sales by sparking interest—with branded cups, regular ministry updates and so on—among the more than 200,000 individuals who are currently being serviced by Pura Vida's commercial vendors.
- Expand awareness of and interest in the Constant Cup subscription program.
- Introduce new merchandise and coffee-related products (for example, canisters, espresso equipment, hot chocolate mix and so on) to encourage incremental purchases and to increase average order size.
- Expand awareness of the affiliate rebate program, which allows retail customers to designate a portion of their individual purchases to their local church or qualified charitable organization.
- More effectively collect and cultivate leads on potential retail customers.

Table 9.2. Pura Vida Management Team

Name	Title	Experience
John Sage	President & CEO, board member	See biographical sketch above.
Greg Forsythe	Chief Operating Officer (COO)	Greg spent more than ten years in senior management positions in the specialty coffee industry. As sales and general manager of Caravali Coffee, he grew a three-million-dollar regional concern into a twenty-three-million-dollar national company. Forsythe brings fifteen-plus years of sales, operations and general management experience with Fortune 100 companies (IBM and PACCAR).
Brian Vinkemulder, CPA	Chief Financial Officer (CFO)	Brian spent more than six years with Ernst & Young, specializing in consumer products and nonprofit industry practice. He has extensive experience in audit, mergers and acquisitions and international practice.
Scott James	Director of Marketing	Scott spent the last several years in high-tech marketing at Microsoft and Visio. Prior to that he did consumer and industry marketing for General Electric.

Table 9.3. Pura Vida Board of Directors

Name	Title	Experience
Ray Conn Cincinnati, Ohio	Founder and Chairman, C&S Contractors	Ray is a serial entrepreneur and founder of a highly successful architecture and construction firm. An owner of multiple Burger King franchises, Ray also brings food and consumer sales experience. He is passionate about education, helping to launch Cincinnati Hills Christian Academy and founding the Service Learning program at Lee University.
Scott Hardman Seattle, Wash.	Managing Director, Alexander Hutton	Scott has extensive experience in finance and management and is a leading figure in the Seattle business community. He also serves on numerous company and charitable boards, including The Salvation Army and World Vision. He is chair of the Washington Governor's Economic Development Finance Authority.
Ken Kierstead Seattle, Wash.	Senior Director of Urban and Global Mission, University Presbyterian Church (UPC)	Ken leads the overall mission vision and programs for UPC. Formerly the executive director for Emerald City Outreach Ministries, he is a leader in the fields of inner-city ministry and urban redevelopment.
Mike Metzger Seattle, Wash.	President & CEO, Performant	Mike brings seventeen years of management, marketing and technical experience, having held senior positions with Real Networks, Microsoft, Heinz and Boeing.
Greg Nelson Seattle, Wash.	Senior Director, Microsoft	Greg is the senior director of Financial Services for Microsoft's MSN Service, leading efforts to build relationships with financial institutions like Schwab and American Express. Greg has an extensive history in the nonprofit world and serves as the chairman of Pura Vida's board.
Paul Olson Minneapolis, Minn.	Trustee, Special Assistant to the President, Bethel Seminary	Paul was a founding executive officer of Sterling Commerce and a veteran of numerous high-tech and financial services companies. A former professional football player, he brings passion and thought to all pursuits and currently devotes energy to charitable activity.

RISKS

Pura Vida Coffee, like any company with a limited operating history, faces many uncertainties and risks.

- **Existing and potential competition.** There are many companies engaged in the sale of specialty coffee, and many of them are well established and pose a potential competitive threat. Some are already operating in one or more of the niche markets that Pura Vida focuses on, such as the sale of shade-grown or organically grown coffees, or the sale of coffee to benefit charitable purposes. In addition, the entry barriers in this industry are relatively low, which opens up the possibility of competition from new entrants as well.

- **Dependence on key personnel.** The company's success is highly dependent, at least in the short term, on its ability to retain the services of key personnel, including John Sage, Greg Forsythe and Brian Vinkemulder. None of these individuals have employment contracts, and the loss of the services of any of them would have an adverse material affect on the company.

- **Lack of adequate internal resources for growth.** The company is not in a position to achieve or sustain growth internally and is still highly dependent on the willingness of outside investors to fund its growth. Thus the possibility always exists that the company will not have the resources to fully implement its growth strategy.

- **Lack of diversification.** Pura Vida is not currently in a position to invest in other ventures, businesses or investment vehicles, or in any other way to diversify its income stream.

CAPITALIZATION FOR GROWTH

What we see described above is highly typical of startup companies: there is a fascinating new idea that has significant moneymaking potential, the idea is currently being tested in the marketplace and is showing some promise, but there are substantial risks, largely due to the company's immaturity and shortage of working capital. The obvious solution is to sell a share of the future profits to an outside investor or group of investors through a private equity placement. But what if the company is constrained by its bylaws to send any and all future profits to a nonprofit foundation? Bylaws can be changed, of course, but what if that foundation is in the process of acquiring a controlling interest in the company, thus foreclosing that possibility? The incentive as a private investor changes dramatically. Given that the law will treat this as a purchase of equity and not as a donation, the investment cannot be deducted as a charitable contribution. Yet for all practical purposes, that is what it is, for the investor will never see a return on that money. Spiritual rewarding, yes, but the investor will not benefit personally, at least not in this lifetime.

Another approach is to sell bonds, which is what John opted to do. He assumed that people would be motivated more by the company's charitable purpose than by the interest rate, so he created a straight debt instrument that promised a relatively modest 6 percent annual return for five years. To his surprise, no one took the bait—not a single investor, no matter how wealthy or how spiritually mature. John was now thoroughly perplexed. The solution to the problem of how to raise outside funding for this company continued to elude him. But then, during a conversation with a prospective investor, the nature of the problem became clear. "The way this deal was structured, it appealed to the heart but not to the head," John says. From the potential investor's perspective, the absolute best-case scenario, "assuming we hit all our numbers," would mean a modest financial return for five years, then the relationship ends. "I realized that these were all 'big idea' guys. It wasn't the money they cared about, it was the ability to participate in something groundbreaking, to be a stakeholder."

John immediately went to work crafting a new way to "package" the investment. The restructured investment involves a long-term debt instrument, or Series A Note, which is sold in units of fifty thousand dollars that will pay an estimated 5.66 percent over a term of five to eight years. Each unit comes with an option, exercisable after all of the Series A Notes are repaid, to purchase ten equity units in the company for a nominal sum. To protect the tax-exempt status of Pura Vida Partners, which will own the balance of the equity in the company, the options can only be exercised and held by a Section 501(c)(3) nonprofit corporation. Accordingly, the prospective buyer of each Series A Note must designate a 501(c)(3) nonprofit corporation to become the owner of those shares. In this way 100 percent of the ownership of Pura Vida Coffee will eventually reside with nonprofit organizations. Furthermore, investors not only receive their principal with interest, but they also can bless their favorite charity by designating it as the owner of the equity units. In other words, the relationship need not end, especially if the investor is actively involved in the designated charity.

John was excited about this financial innovation and expected that he would soon find receptive investors. But to his dismay he continued to strike out everywhere he went. He was now down to about six weeks of cash. He was traveling extensively, telling the Pura Vida story and speaking to anyone who would listen. But still he could not convince anyone to part with their money. After more than a year of hitting this brick wall, John was discouraged—thoroughly discouraged. It was winter, he was in Chicago, and he had to be in Indianapolis for a breakfast meeting with a prospective investor the next morning. That evening as he began the drive to Indiana, a massive ice storm caused two tractor-trailer trucks to collide, shutting down the interstate. What should have been a three-and-a-half-hour drive turned into an all-nighter. It looked certain that he would miss his appointment. Sorely disappointed again, he called his wife on his cell phone—and wept. Looking back, John recalls, "There was something about that moment of complete despair, something that reminded me, as those moments have on several other occasions, to start trusting more in God to meet my specific needs, to become less self-reliant."

He arrived that morning tired, unshaven and in no mood to go through the usual routine. Instead he simply carried on a polite conversation with the man and gave no pitch. But the man insisted, and John shared the Pura Vida story, the unvarnished version. The man drank it in, asked a few questions and after a pause said, "Well, this just became the most expensive breakfast of my life." He invested thirty thousand dollars. Five months later John had raised the half-million dollars necessary to keep the company afloat. Eleven months later the figure was up to almost one million, and by mid-summer 2003 John expects the investment will be fully subscribed at two million dollars. That money will be used to finance operation and growth until the end of 2004, at which time the company expects to be consistently profitable. Assuming the offering does become fully subscribed, Pura Vida Partners will own a minimum of 60 percent of the outstanding shares. Chris and John are also hoping that many investors will designate Pura Vida Partners as the recipient of those equity units, thereby increasing the share of the profits that will flow through to the ministries in Costa Rica.

THE MINISTRY STORY

The Pura Vida ministry has three main components. First, there is a social justice component that is an important part of the company's purpose. Roughly 75 percent of the coffee sold by Pura Vida is "fair trade" coffee, and they expect that figure to reach 100 percent by the end of summer 2003. Fair trade coffee is sourced, roasted and transported through a coffee cooperative that is able to eliminate eleven steps in the production-to-delivery process. The removal of so many intermediaries enables the cooperative to pay the farmers a higher rate for their beans ($1.26 per pound, almost double the current commodity price for coffee) without requiring an increase in price at the retail end. John believes that the exclusive focus on fair trade coffee is another company distinctive and an important selling point, especially on college campuses.

The second component is the income raised for Pura Vida Partners and other charitable organizations through (1) direct contributions and grants, (2) the funds raised and rebates paid to ministry partners and affiliates for coffee sales, and (3) the dividends paid to its stockholders (all of whom are nonprofit organizations). As figure 9.1 shows, the most significant benefit thus far has been the money raised directly for Pura Vida Partners from individuals, corporations and foundations (direct contributions and grants). By the end of 2002, over four hundred thousand dollars had been raised this way, thanks largely to the increased awareness generated by Pura Vida Coffee. This figure is expected to grow to about one million dollars *annually* by 2010. In addition to financial assistance, over a dozen churches have sent short-term ministry teams to Costa Rica to assist in the work being done there, and this trend is expected to continue as well. Another one hundred thousand dollars has been raised through fundraisers and rebates to support the work of its ministry partners and affiliates, and this figure is expected to reach almost five hundred thousand dollars per year by 2010. And finally, John predicts that by 2010 annual dividends paid to investor charities will reach $1.3 million. Given that Pura Vida Partners will own a minimum of 60 percent of the outstanding shares, this will be another important source of income for that ministry.

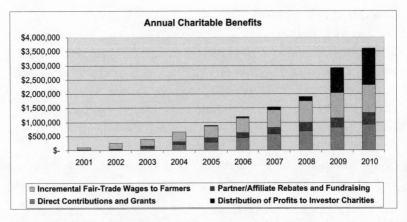

Figure 9.1. Annual ministry benefits

The third ministry component is the direct impact Pura Vida Partners is having in the lives of at-risk children in Costa Rica. Chris shares many of these stories in his monthly newsletter, which is available on the company website. He sees his role and that of the volunteers from his church as one of partnering with indigenous and faith-centered ministries to provide a wide range of services aimed at meeting the physical, emotional and spiritual needs of kids who are surrounded by violence, prostitution and drug use. The ministries work in neighborhoods that even the police avoid. Most of the children are malnourished and suffering from disease, infection and other physical ailments. Without these ministries, few would receive education or technical training of any kind. Chris describes it as a strategy of breadth and depth: breadth because they help in a wide variety of areas, such as kids clubs, computer training centers and soup kitchens; depth because it is about more than just meeting immediate physical needs. They also want to build a sense of self-esteem and spiritual hunger in the kids.

Chris becomes quite passionate when talking about the importance of self-esteem. Remember that these are children who see little reason to hope for a better future. One manifestation of this hopelessness is a disinterest in learning, so one of the first problems these ministries must solve is to motivate the kids to learn. Chris has found computers to be an invaluable tool for this. The kids can do anything on a computer, from creating greeting cards or PowerPoint presentations to flying a plane or riding a motorcycle. "The self-esteem that is brought into the lives of these kids when they start to see a connection between learning and life is amazing," says Chris. "They gain a new vision for who they can become, what their life might be about." There is enough history now that Chris has also seen many of these young people become leaders in their schools and in their communities. He is now trying to create links between these kids and the newer children. In particular he is looking to them to help the younger ones find jobs.

Finally, not far from the kids club, a new church now meets, as families in this neighborhood are believing for the first time that Christ is alive and that he cares deeply about them. The outreach has been transforming for the members of Chris's church as well. In addition to the twenty or so who volunteer on a weekly or biweekly basis, the entire church organizes and participates in an annual Christmas party in the community. Chris's bridge appears to be firmly in place.

ANALYSIS AND CONCLUSIONS

Pura Vida Coffee is an excellent illustration of the power of business. Not only can businesses be a source of income for ministries, but they can often find ways to get ministry leverage out of their resources through alliances formed with other ministries and/or through the increased awareness that they can generate about the needs of others. In the case of Pura Vida, "What may begin as an economic relationship with the customer turns into something much more," John says. It also illustrates the point we made earlier in the book that a GCC need not necessarily locate in a developing country. In fact, that may be counterproductive. Instead, John Sage and other kingdom professionals are finding ways to tap into the economic power of the United

States and other industrialized countries and use it as a pipeline to move critical resources to the less-developed world.

Pura Vida is well managed and well governed, with adequate leadership in place in both the United States and Costa Rica. The board of directors is made up of respected people from both the business and the ministry communities. The possibility of an adverse event leading to an ownership change has been minimized by having the ownership rest with Pura Vida Partners and other nonprofit corporations. But no matter how professionally managed and governed Pura Vida may be, the founders are learning that ultimately it is "not by might nor by power" but by the Spirit that this effort will succeed (see Zech 4:6).

QUESTIONS FOR REVIEW

1. What were the important stages of John's preparation? Chris's preparation? Given where they are now, what could they have done better to prepare? Do you think Chris's MBA degree is being wasted?

2. What lessons can be learned from John's early career? What did he do well, and what could he have done better?

3. When you imagine your dream job, does it look more like John's or Chris's? Assuming God has called you to do something like that, what steps should you take to prepare?

4. How does the combination of Pura Vida Coffee and Pura Vida Partners measure up to the questions in the sidebar "Assessing the Viability of a GCC" (pp. 94-95)? What are the principle strengths and weaknesses?

10
THE PIONEERING ALLIANCE

GLOBAL ENGINEERING AND MANAGEMENT SOLUTIONS

ESTABLISHED: 1989

LOCATION: Offices and equity investments throughout Asia, the Middle East and North Africa

EMPLOYEES: 350, including the equity holdings

PROJECTED REVENUE (2003): $10 million, including the equity holdings

MISSION STATEMENT: To start and grow world-class business operations on behalf of our U.S.A.-based holding company and our multinational clients, and to recruit and train our management and investor teams around a common shared set of Christian values and ethics.

OVERVIEW

Global Engineering and Management Solutions (GEMS; not its real name) provides a broad range of services for companies seeking to invest abroad. These services include feasibility studies, site selection, market research, licensing and registration, human resource management, equipment acquisition and importation, and other essential steps toward successfully doing business in a foreign country. GEMS is made up of a multicultural team of kingdom professionals from New Zealand, South America, England and the United States. It currently has six regional offices and equity holdings in an additional ten companies in major cities throughout the 10/40 Window. To date, it has helped establish almost twenty factories that collectively employ more than two thousand nationals and generate $200 million in revenue per year. Many of the factories are located in unreached cities and are themselves managed by teams of kingdom professionals. As in any portfolio, not all of these companies have been successful both spiritually and financially. But the experience gained from this mixed record has helped the company founder identify a list of "best practices" that is itself a major contribution to future efforts in this area.

PERSONAL BACKGROUND

John Larson (not his real name) had the good fortune of being brought up in a loving, Christian home. God's desire to have eternal fellowship with people from every race, tongue and tribe was a message that was continually reinforced. As a boy John had many positive crosscultural experiences, such as living in a racially mixed neighborhood in Chicago, having relatives who were missionaries in Japan and belonging to a missions-minded church. His family's home was a regular gathering place for after-church activities and a resting place for visiting missionaries. At the age of six he accepted Christ during a backyard Bible club, and from that day forward his top priority was to serve God by telling others about Jesus. His favorite books as a young boy were missionary biographies, and by the time he was eleven he never hesitated to reply "missionary" when asked, "What do you want to be when you grow up?"

As a teenager John led evangelism classes at his church and organized door-to-door evangelism trips in the local neighborhoods. He started and led a wide range of youth Bible studies and helped organize Christian conferences for local high schoolers. He was an avid athlete but preferred playing on teams that had an evangelistic purpose. His enthusiasm for evangelism was contagious, his leadership skills were quite natural, and wherever he went there always seemed to be a group of close friends who were "on fire" about spreading the good news. Even so, he was the only one out of about fourteen hundred kids in his high school yearbook who said he wanted to one day be a missionary.

After high school John accepted a full scholarship—in academics, he is quick to point out, not sports—at Texas Christian University (TCU). He majored in religion and minored in philosophy and also played on the school's basketball team and belonged to the Baptist Student Union (BSU). A person with boundless energy, John excelled in everything that he put his mind to.

Yet his ultimate goal was to learn about God's will for his life. He had no desire to pastor a church but was equally certain about his calling into ministry. As part of his search for God's will, he committed to reading one missionary biography per week for the first five months of college. Soon he was feeling a tug toward assisting Chinese Christians, and he began studying Chinese and arranging to have a Chinese roommate.

The first woman John ever dated was one he met in his sophomore year through BSU. Though she was athletic, intelligent and beautiful, what attracted him most was Diane's uncommon commitment to evangelism and missions. His father recalls that John's first comment about her to the family was that she was "the most spiritual girl I have ever met." Her goal was to become a medical doctor and to use those skills as a vehicle for bringing the gospel to her native country of Iran. Soon they were dating a little and partnering in ministry a lot. Diane was the Bible study coordinator and helped start ten studies. John, now president of BSU, was spearheading new sports and dormitory ministries and outreach efforts to senior citizens, the poor and the homeless. By the time he graduated, BSU had grown into the largest student religious organization on campus.

After graduation John went to Hong Kong to study Chinese for the summer, then to Taiwan to play professional basketball for a Chinese team. Because he was only the second foreigner ever to play in the league, John had an excellent opportunity to learn the language. However, while he was making good progress with the language, he was still unclear about what God wanted him to do next. So that Christmas he returned to the States to attend InterVarsity's Urbana Student Mission Convention. It was at this conference that God impressed on him the opportunities that were available as a marketplace messenger of the gospel and the need for him to get more professional training. Later, upon fulfilling his basketball contract (and turning down a request for an extension), he moved to Boston where he was accepted into Harvard/Tufts's two-year program in law and diplomacy. Before returning to the States, however, he spent another summer taking language classes in Hong Kong, where, as "luck" would have it, Diane was also spending the summer as part of a nursing internship.

Diane graduated the following spring, and that summer they were married in a ceremony on the TCU campus. They settled in Boston since John was already living there, and Diane began working part time as a nurse while also studying for her medical school entrance exams. The study paid off with an acceptance into the University of Texas Medical School. The couple then moved to Houston, where John went to work for a multinational maker of oilfield equipment. He advanced quickly within the company and soon was overseeing the sales and field engineering assignments in Latin America and Asia, and providing in-house legal support for their operations in China. He also enrolled in an executive MBA program at the University of Houston.

John and Diane had a unique marriage. Their busy schedules were matched by their boundless energy and their passion for ministry. John recalls that Diane "lived and breathed missions." At the medical school, she helped lead a Bible study group of about fifty students, residents and interns. They continued to stay deeply involved in ministry to Chinese students. John recalls, for example, inviting about twenty Chinese students for Thanksgiving one year and making a soy-flavored gravy for the turkey to give it a little Chinese flair. Once or twice each month they took roughly forty students to different places around Houston and occasionally organized longer excursions, like one trip to Colorado to attend an InterVarsity Christian Fellowship conference during Christmas break.

The oil market slump in the mid-1980s hit John's company hard, and his employment future began looking grim. With the ink barely dry on his MBA, John took advantage of a business trip in China to hand out some résumés. A large multinational firm offered him a job as senior marketing representative for their joint venture in China. Within eighteen months he was overseeing all of that division's activities and its multimillion-dollar budget.

In some respects, this was everything John was working toward. He was fluent in the national language and had the credibility of one of America's largest corporations behind him. Many of his coworkers, customers and teammates were hearing about Jesus for the first time, and people were committing their lives to him on a regular basis. John's company-paid, executive-worthy apartment became a way station for traveling expatriates, especially missionaries passing through who needed advice or simply a break from the dirt, noise and foreignness of the country. According to his guest book, at least twelve hundred people stayed overnight or longer over this three-year period.

In terms of their family life, however, it was not easy. Diane's responsibilities as a medical student limited her ability to live in China, and John estimates they were apart 85 percent of the time during the first year. Eventually they were able to settle into a routine in which they alternated between China and Texas. During her stays in China, Diane worked in two different hospitals and began to grow in her own appreciation for the Chinese people and culture. She began dreaming of one day establishing a Christian teaching hospital and an emergency medical response team in Asia.

This back-and-forth routine was manageable—at least they were together more often—but when she was accepted into University of Chicago's premier, three-year program in emergency medicine, they knew they had little choice but to return full time to America. John's employer offered him several attractive alternative positions, including one in its Chicago office, but he decided instead to buy a small, two-year-old company named Global Engineering and Management Solutions (GEMS) as a way to stay involved in mainland China.

COMPANY HISTORY

Phase one. The year was now 1989. The Soviet Union was disintegrating and new countries with strange-sounding names like Kyrgyzstan and Uzbekistan were springing up almost overnight. Governments were being toppled in Poland, Romania, the Philippines and elsewhere. Soon China would come close to erupting before the government stepped in and reaffirmed its control. Suddenly everything everyone thought they knew about Central and East Asia was obsolete. The economic picture, which was never terribly clear in the first place, was now cloudier and even more uncertain. Businesses were being invited to bring their capital and know-how to these unpredictable countries, but few people understood the countries well enough to reach the necessary level of comfort. The few attempts made were almost always disappointing failures.

It is fair to say that John was called and uniquely prepared for a time such as this. Fluent in two of the world's dominant languages, educated in law, diplomacy and business, and passionate about seeing light break into dark places, he had the skills, the patience and the guileless motives to be an ambassador for Christian-owned businesses. But to his dismay GEMS's principle business partner—a group of tentmaker missionaries called LTN based in East Asia—was doing little real business.[1] Annual revenues were rarely more than $100,000 in spite of the eighty people "working" for the company. LTN was interested only in recruiting, training and placing Christian professionals within China and the surrounding countries. With only a small pool of willing Christian professionals to draw from, in practice this became an effort to create what were little more than fronts for full-time missionaries. John believed they could do better. He believed it was possible not only to bring world-class businesses into these countries, but also to find qualified teams of kingdom professionals to manage them.

The company's first experience in a former Soviet republic in the early 1990s is a typical example of how GEMS and LTN worked together. After negotiating with the government to be the first Western corporation allowed into the country, they opened an office in the capital city and staffed it with three donor-supported tentmaker-missionaries from two mission agencies. They spent the next year raising eighty thousand dollars in grant money from international development agencies to build and staff an educational center, which allowed additional expatriate workers to join the effort. All told there were fifteen expatriates from five countries and three agencies who were offering intensive training in English, business and finance.

As an effort to plant churches, this was a phenomenal success. Within a year the team was discipling eighty-six national believers, and by last count more than four thousand believers were fellowshiping in several churches in the community. But by other measures this effort was a disappointment. Few lasting jobs were created, only one small spin-off business lasted more than a couple of years, and the combined effort never was able to support itself financially. LTN and GEMS eventually agreed to go their separate ways, but during the three years of partnership, John was able to tap the connections and relationships that had been established by these (now more than one hundred) agent/missionaries and turn them into actual clients. In the process GEMS quickly became the single biggest source of income for LTN.

Phase two. Once the relationship was severed, the first thing John did was broaden GEMS's business plan by offering consulting and management services, specializing in equipment and engineering contracts, to a wide range of technology-intensive companies. With the help of LTN representatives, he identified Chinese business owners and key government leaders who would benefit from a Western technology partner. He often brought groups of these people to the States to help them build relationships with potential technology partners. That first year he brokered several significant manufacturing equipment deals and the company recorded more than three million dollars in sales. This in turn enabled them to hire more staff and open additional offices in East and Central Asia. LTN also benefited handsomely from the deals. Over the next couple of years sales exceeded ten million dollars per year, and the company began making its first equity investments in East Asia. By 1993 John had helped start more than a dozen factories ranging in valuation from $1.5 million to $3.5 million.

John then began refocusing the business away from brokering technology deals toward more direct investment and headhunting. As part of his headhunting efforts, he initiated a six-month "internship" program to help those with foreign language skills learn more about international business and foreign investment. Missionaries merely looking for an entry strategy were not welcome. Instead John was interested in those who genuinely wanted to serve the Chinese and other nationalities by bringing in foreign investment. The interns worked under his supervision for anywhere from six to twenty-four months, learning the ins and outs of international business and foreign direct investment. After observing and coaching them for that length of time, not only did John have a good sense of their abilities, but he also had a ready source of kingdom professionals who could manage some of the factories, at least during interim periods while a global search was conducted for a permanent replacement.

It is important to note that GEMS does not work exclusively with Christian-owned companies. Bringing foreign investment, helping the client navigate all the hurdles and finding qualified management and staff to manage the newly constructed factory is what John does for a living. When one of his interns or another kingdom professional fits the bill, he happily makes the connection. But his first priority is to provide the best service possible for his clients. In an ideal world, all John's clients would be kingdom-minded business owners who desire to see their businesses bless people in the least-evangelized parts of the world. But many Christian business owners have not yet been challenged to look beyond the impact their business can have locally.

One noteworthy exception is XYZ Corporation (not its real name). In 1994 a large American corporation approached John about helping it establish a manufacturing plant in China. It just so happened that the top candidate for technology partner was XYZ Corporation, a GCC based in the Middle East. Once the match was made and the joint venture was formed, John proceeded to register and supervise the factory construction. With the help of some demographic research provided by a mission agency, they ultimately located the plant in a district heavily populated by an unreached Muslim people group. Because of John's impeccable credibility and experience, he was given a free hand in recruiting the management team: a multiethnic, multinational, fully business-supported team of kingdom professionals. Within twelve months this factory was employing more than two hundred people and exceeding all expectations for profits and sales.

Not everything went well, however. Soon after the company was launched, a family emergency forced the human resources manager to return to the States, which severely undermined their efforts to hire Muslims. Furthermore, the general manager's marriage and spiritual accountability relationships began to come unraveled. About a year later the wife and children were living in the States, he was no longer attending church, and the ministry was essentially moribund. John was not at all happy, and he tried to use his influence as a member of the board of directors to have the general manager replaced. Not all the board members were in sympathy with John's ministry goals, however, and even the owner of XYZ Corporation, in a rare difference of opinion, sided with the other board members to keep the current manager. This experience, along with the experience gained from his other experiments with blending business and missions, have led to a list of what John believes are "best practices" for managing and governing GCCs, a list we will look at momentarily.

Satan strikes! Meanwhile Diane finished her medical training and landed her "dream job" as an emergency-room physician in North Carolina. The Larsons and GEMS's twelve interns and employees all moved to North Carolina (to accommodate her new job) and hardly missed a beat as they began to minister to the local Chinese population, especially by reaching out to medical interns at the hospital. In fact, not only were the GEMS interns and employees living in the Larsons' home, but over those next few years some twenty Chinese students lived there during their six-month medical internships.

Not long after moving to North Carolina, Diane received a call from an old high school sweetheart. Recently divorced, he was looking for some help from Diane. What began perhaps as an innocent desire to help a hurting friend quickly grew into something much more. Feelings that had been long suppressed began to awaken, and Diane decided it was best to keep the phone calls a secret. Over the next seven months the phone calls became more regular and the relationship progressed from an emotional affair to a physical one. John had no idea anything was wrong. His work required him to travel a lot—by his own estimation he was gone 25 to 35 percent of the time—so it was natural for Diane to take care of all the personal finances. John knew nothing about the lengthy telephone calls or the money she was secreting away for her planned separation and divorce.

That all changed on Easter Sunday 1995. About nineteen months after the first phone call, Diane announced that she wanted a separation. Over the next few months of marriage counseling, the reasons she gave were almost all financial. Owning a business, especially a startup like GEMS, can be a nerve-wracking experience. As the keeper of the personal finances she was keenly aware of how precarious things would get from time to time. Gradually her priorities began to change and she began wishing for a more stable lifestyle, one more befitting a medical doctor. She accused John of being "obsessed" with the Great Commission. Never did she admit to the affair she was having with another man, and John remained clueless about it until he discovered two intimate letters. "It was the worst day of my life," he recalls.

In addition to seeking help from counselors and pastors, John turned to his personal accountability group. Though not connected to any missionary sending agency, John still believed it was important to have spiritual accountability, and over the years he had assembled a group of five men who were committed to keeping him from straying. Even they had been blindsided by the infidelity because, until the very end of the relationship, Diane appeared to be committed to her faith and deeply involved in ministry. Collectively they told him to cease all travel, cut back his workload and give first priority to repairing his relationship with Diane. He followed their advice, but by then it was too late. She was not only already divorced emotionally, but it was obvious from the letters that she had determined it was God's will for her to leave. Finally, eighteen months after the affair started and six months after John found out about it, Diane moved out.

It is fair to say that up until then John had lived a charmed life in the sense that his dreams always seemed to come true. Now, for the first time in his life, he was personally experiencing the full reality and intensity of the battle being waged between God and Satan. He was, in his words, an "emotional robot" during this period. The company floundered and not a single contract was implemented. All he could do was write letters—one, sometimes two a day—to Diane, telling her how much he loved her and wanted her back. The accountability group had agreed that John should not date until at least six months after she remarried. Regrettably she did remarry, and six months later in a private, deeply personal moment during Promise Keepers' Million Man March, the group laid hands on him, prayed and released him from his obligations to Diane. He now felt free to shut down his U.S. operations and return to China.

Phase three. It was not long before John was supervising the construction and staffing of a new factory, a subsidiary of a U.S.-based multinational. He accepted the position of general manager and, starting with no employees and no purchase orders, grew it into a five-hundred-employee, six-million-dollar operation within twelve months. Its production levels far exceeded that of a sister factory in the Philippines that had nearly three times as many employees, and it received two design awards, including one as "overall best manufacturing startup in China" by Arthur Andersen.

What the financial audits did not show, however, was the spiritual impact. The factory, which was managed by a team of kingdom professionals, was seeing an average of ten conversions per month, and within five months four new house churches had been planted. By every measure of economic and spiritual impact, John views this as one of his most successful GCCs. However, after a fundamental shift in corporate policy a year later that moved all personnel and marketing functions back to the States, John resigned his position and poured himself once again into GEMS.

In the summer of 2000, several factory startups later, John married a long-time friend who shares a passion for sports and for the Chinese people. John first met this former member of the U.S. Olympic softball team on a basketball court in China, and they discovered they had many other interests in common. For example, like John, she has a long history in China and enjoys the respect of many of the country's leading figures. Likewise, her respect and love for the Chinese people is unrestrained, and her management style is a model of grace and empowerment. The two recognize the dangers of juggling two high-intensity careers and have committed to doing as much business travel together as possible. They have set a target of being together at least 85 percent of each year. (Setting a measurable goal was no doubt John's idea.)

Today GEMS has six semi-autonomous offices located throughout the 10/40 Window. Each office is staffed by kingdom professionals who have formal accountability relationships with churches or misions agencies. To date, the company has helped establish almost twenty factories, and there are three more in various stages of completion. Between them the factories represent more than two thousand jobs created and $200 million in annual revenues, almost all of it from overseas sales.

THE MINISTRY STORY

Not all of the factories established by GEMS are managed by kingdom professionals. John goes to great lengths to find the best people for the job, period. Often they are people drawn from the local talent pool: college educated and eager to work for a foreign corporation. But other times, either because of the specific skill sets required or the challenges related to managing a subsidiary of a Western corporation in a foreign country, kingdom professionals can have an edge. All told, about half of the factories have, or at least had, kingdom professionals in the management level. Not all succeeded as GCCs, as we have seen. Some were hugely successful by some measures but not others. But, especially if we include the six regional GEMS offices, we can see why John is still the most respected and widely sought-after adviser in organizing, managing and governing GCCs.

John has encapsulated much of that expertise in a set of best practices that he believes will maximize the chances of both economic and spiritual success. Readers will notice many similarities between his list and our own recommendations in chapters five and six. This was not coincidental. We began our research with his best practices in hand and tested them against our own sample of companies to see which ones are universally important and which are specific to his manufacturing experience. Below is his list of best practices, as well as our responses based on our own research.

- *There should be a missions strategy coordinator on the management team and board of directors*. This person's primary concern will be to network with local church leaders, creating joint strategies for evangelism, discipleship and church planting, and ensuring that the GCC meets its ministry goals. To the degree that this person is benefiting the company through community relations and employee development, his or her salary can legitimately be considered a company expense.

  Our response. We have likewise concluded that one or more representatives from the missions community should be on the board. This of course assumes that the company has a functioning board of directors. Not all kingdom professionals have gone to the trouble of cultivating advisers and organizing a board, usually to the detriment of the business and/or ministry. Having a company employee dedicated to the purpose of community and employee development may at first sound like a luxury that few GCCs can afford. But some companies not related to GEMS, including the Silk Road Handicraft Company, have employed variations of this approach, sometimes giving the person a human resources title or an unofficial title like "company intercessor." When we consider that no company achieves its maximum potential without prayer, an argument can be made that it makes good business and ministry sense to have a person whose full-time job is to pray and to cultivate a culture of prayer within the company. Effective prayer requires getting to know everyone associated with the company: management, employees, customers, suppliers and the surrounding community.

- *The expatriates in the business should be spiritually accountable to a church or mission agency.* Moreover, the accountability group and the GCC should have a written contract that specifies the conditions of employment.

Our response. Accountability relationships with a mission agency can be problematic, as it connotes "missionary" to almost anyone who finds out about it. And people will find out. Non-Westerners in particular are naturally bold about asking questions about an expatriate's income source(s), motives, affiliations and so on. The most credible and morally dilemma-free kingdom professionals are those who, like John Larson and Jeff Nolan, depend entirely on their businesses for their livelihoods and are accountable to individual Christians, not agencies.

- *GCCs need to be managed by a team of kingdom professionals.* Stand-alone kingdom professionals have limited effectiveness. Kingdom professionals should comprise a majority of the management team, at least. Care should be taken that there is no one at the management level who is antagonistic to the holistic purpose of the company.

Our response. To this we would add that, at a minimum, the position of CEO or general manager should be held by a kingdom professional. This is probably implied in John's point, but it should be added for clarity. Unless the buck stops at a kingdom professional's desk, the company itself will not be a central part of a missions strategy.

- *Ideally the team should be composed of people from several ethnic backgrounds (at least three).* Not only will a multiethnic, multicultural team have fewer language or cultural limitations, but also such an environment creates opportunities for Christians to model grace and forgiveness crossculturally, something that is a completely foreign concept in many cultures.

Our response. Again we agree. The apostle Paul always worked with multicultural teams, and a strong case can be made that it was more than a coincidence; it was an intentional part of his strategy.

- *Two separate people should lead the ministry and the business.* This ensures that both areas of responsibility are given maximum attention.

Our response. We are not ready to endorse such a blanket statement, as we have found that some of the most successful and effective GCCs have one person leading both. John is correct that the business and ministry both require competent leadership, and that it is often helpful to assign separate people to these roles. However, tensions between the business and ministry are almost inevitable, and there needs to be one person who ultimately has the final say. A board of directors can often serve this function, but that may not always be practical because sometimes those decisions must be made on the spot.

- *There is a business plan and a Great Commission plan in place that establish ambitious, culturally achievable goals.* Ideally there will be a synergistic relationship between the business and ministry that maximizes the effectiveness of each.

Our response. We have developed this point at greater length in chapter five.

- *Compensation for the core management team should be performance-based and drawn from the company.* Managers are more likely to make good decisions when their salaries are based on performance. GEMS does allow some nonmanagement people who focus primarily on the ministry activities to receive some or most of their compensation from nonprofit groups.

Our response. We are in total agreement with the first part of this, but the second part raises major concerns. While John adequately addresses the legal issues raised when mixing for-profit and nonprofit activities, there are ethical questions as to whether the "nonmanagement people" are little more than undercover missionaries. Some evangelical Christians have rationalized this tactic and can even give biblical support, but as evidenced in the recent exposé on this approach in *Time* magazine, most people, including many evangelicals, see it as dishonest and hypocritical. Can a GCC hire part-time expatriate employees? Absolutely. Can those employees also do part-time community work and be paid by a nonprofit? Sure. But care needs to be taken to avoid the appearance that the company is merely a front for missionaries.

- *A significant portion of a GCC's production should be for export markets.* Not only does the inflow of foreign exchange provide political leverage for the company, but given that sales are less dependent on local leaders, it also helps reduce the potential problems of bribery and corruption. Selling internationally also forces the company to stay up-to-date in its expertise, resources and standards.

  Our response. John makes a strong defense for focusing on export markets. There are additional benefits as well, as we elaborated in chapter three. However, there are instances when production for the domestic market can be justified, as long as it is something that is currently being imported heavily by that country.

- *A GCC should have a formal employee training program on business ethics.* The company should also have written policies or guidelines regarding how to handle ethically ambiguous situations. (See the sidebar "GEMS's Employee Anticorruption Guidelines.")

  Our response. There is nothing more we can say about this, other than "we agree."

- *The GCC leadership team should be prescreened in areas of both business and ministry competencies.* One screening program that John likes is that which is conducted roughly twice a year by the Center of Entrepreneurship and Economic Development (CEED).

- *Our response.* The three-week CEED seminars are good introductions to the power of integrating business and missions. During the seminar, students are introduced to a variety of topics related to crosscultural ministry, crosscultural business and the theology of "business as mission." The students are also expected to form teams and produce a business plan (or a good outline of one). It gives students a snapshot of what it takes to

GEMS'S EMPLOYEE ANTICORRUPTION GUIDELINES

GEMS requires its employees to follow a four-step process whenever there is a possibility of bribery, corruption or kickbacks. Each step must be followed in the order it is presented here. If all four questions are not answered with "no," then the proposed action should not be taken. These guidelines are taught to all employees at least annually in all GEMS-related companies.

1. Does the proposed action violate the U.S. Federal Corrupt Practices Act? The 1976 Federal Corrupt Practices Act (FCPA) has no territorial limits. It prohibits any U.S.-based company from giving gifts to government-related officials when the gift is given in direct anticipation of getting a contract or significant business. Violation is a criminal act. GEMS's policy is that any gift more than fifty dollars to any person (not just a government-related official) connected to a potential new business contract must be approved by both John Larson and GEMS's legal department.

2. Does the proposed action create any feelings of discomfort? Whenever a GEMS employee is approached with what may be a possible bribe or kickback, it must be brought to the attention of his or her supervisor. After discussing the situation, if *either* one has an uncomfortable feeling about it, the proposed action cannot be followed through. These discussions must be documented for future reference.

3. Is the proposed action transparent to all directly related parties? Corruption, bribes or kickbacks all require secrecy. Therefore, an easy way to tell a legal from an illegal act is to ask, "Is something being hidden from the other parties?" The employee must make sure that all affected parties are aware of the action.

4. Does the proposed action reflect the Golden Rule: "Do unto others as you want them to do to you"? Employees are encouraged to put themselves in other people's shoes (for example, buyer instead of seller), then examine whether they have any negative feelings. Employees are also encouraged to put themselves in the position of other parties that might be affected.

succeed in this context. By the end of the seminar each student has a better understanding of his or her strengths and weaknesses. Therefore, as a screening tool we agree with John that this is useful. An alternative three-month internship run by Evangelistic Commerce is also a valuable screening and networking tool.

ANALYSIS AND CONCLUSION

There is good reason why John has become the standard-setter for other kingdom professionals. He has proven that it is possible to create world-class businesses that also have a significant kingdom impact. He sees no conflict between his passions for business and missions and has achieved significant results in both areas by, for example, creating thousands of jobs and personally leading hundreds of people to Christ. The story also illustrates the tremendous cost that can arise when Satan feels threatened. The personal toll in terms of the divorce is incalculable, and the wound is still healing.

Sadly, John's was not the only case of divorce we encountered during our research. This raised at least a few questions for us, questions that we were not able to pursue in any depth, given our lack of training in this area. For example, did Diane not feel the same sense of ownership of GEMS and its vision? According to John, she was deeply involved in running the business. But was she, perhaps, subtly treated as a junior partner? Or was her new medical career simply more rewarding, given that she was now able to compete for attention? This problem seems to occur whether or not both spouses work for the company. But alas, we are only speculating here.

In preparation for the work he is now doing John spent years learning and growing under the spiritual mentorship of godly men and women. Furthermore, his professional and ministry skills are the result of extensive education and experience. Aspiring kingdom professionals would do well to follow this same pattern, treating everything about their present circumstances as an opportunity for growth and learning.

QUESTIONS FOR REVIEW

1. What were the important stages of John Larson's ministry preparation?

His business preparation? In retrospect, what could he have done better?

2. What steps, if any, are you taking to find God's will for your life?

3. In your opinion, was the GEMS-LTN partnership in the former Soviet Union a success or failure?

4. What do you think was the fundamental cause of the affair and the divorce?

5. What is your opinion about the list of best practices? Which do you think are essential? Nonessential?

6. What is your opinion of his policy of requiring accountability contracts with mission agencies? Of his willingness to allow some employees to draw donor support?

11

THE NONCONFORMING GCC

GATEWAY TELECOMMUNICATIONS SERVICES

ESTABLISHED: 1995

LOCATION: Headquartered in the United States

EMPLOYEES: Four employees and nineteen representatives in fifteen countries

REVENUE (BEFORE SALE OF COMPANY): $2 million

MISSION STATEMENT: To establish legitimacy of presence through excellence in business so that both profitability and messages of the kingdom will be carried to the uttermost corners of the earth.

OVERVIEW

Gateway Telecommunications Services (GTS) provides customized telecommunications services to the hospitality, tourism and telecommunications industries. From its corporate headquarters in the United States, it oversees a global network of nineteen sales agents, many of whom are kingdom professionals. Seven of the kingdom professionals are lay leaders from the national churches who are getting ministry leverage from their association with a U.S.-based corporation. Five are expatriates who have come through mission agencies and are various shades of kingdom professional and missionary in disguise. The rest are people who are in various pre-belief stages in their spiritual journeys.

We have lightheartedly referred to this as a nonconforming Great Commission Company because, while the agents themselves are doing pioneering work, the company has asserted little control into those areas and is largely facilitative in nature. Similarly, while the company is open to creating alliances with mission agencies and churches, stakeholders have no formal role in the governance of the company. In short, it does not fit cleanly in any category.

PERSONAL BACKGROUND

Nathan Jenkins was ten years old when his mother accepted Christ and, as he puts it, started "dragging me and my brother to church." But in spite of the initial resistance, within weeks he was growing more interested in God, and he began reading the Bible. It was "neat," he says, to learn more about God. Soon Nathan was responding to an altar call at church and taking his new relationship with Christ seriously. For example, after learning in Sunday school that the principle of tithing applied to his *time* as well as his money, he began spending roughly 1.6 hours per day in quiet time with the Lord. He often wrote sermons during his daily devotions, and by the time he was fifteen he was invited by his church to deliver the Sunday evening message from time to time.

An important influence during his teen years was a man named Don Witmer, a tough, red-haired former longshoreman who had a spontaneous style of discipleship that fit well with Nathan's own restless personality. Don became a spiritual mentor to Nathan, studying books with him, attending prayer meetings with him and bringing him each month to meetings of what eventually grew to become Campus Crusade for Christ. A nonserious but likeable student, Nathan sums up his high school years as "standing out as a Christian, going deep and being discipled." He formed Bible clubs at his school and practiced his sermons there. His interest in writing eventually led him to Wheaton College, where he was part of the school's last class of writing majors. (He jokingly refers to himself as "the last writing major from Wheaton," speculating that he finished last in Wheaton's last class of writing majors.)

Nathan was part of the football team's backup squad for two years until a knee injury prompted him to quit and become the college newspaper's sportswriter instead. He also had a radio show on the school's station that was cancelled after three airings because of his unwillingness to conform to the show's format. (According to Nathan, they did not appreciate his "entrepreneurial spontaneity.") In the end, the things that held his interest the most during college were the ministries and the spiritual nourishment that he received there. He remembers being a "sponge" in the classroom and pouring himself into various teaching and evangelistic ministries in inner-city Chicago.

One event that would have a profound impact on the direction of his life was an informal gathering at the beginning of his senior year with some students who had just returned from a summer-long ministry with Campus Crusade for Christ. The news that they led some one hundred college kids to Christ was a bombshell for Nathan. "I couldn't believe it," he recalls. "I was stunned. I thought, *You've got to be kidding; people are that eager to turn to Christ?*" Before long he was being coached on how to share the "Four Spiritual Laws" in casual settings. He joined Campus Crusade on trips to the University of Chicago and, to his amazement, began seeing people accept Christ. "At first I couldn't believe that those University of Chicago kids would listen to someone from Wheaton talk about God," he says. But what he learned was that at some level almost everyone is curious about God and many are open to talking about him, if asked.

After college Nathan joined the Navy and became a fighter pilot. At first blush, the military may not seem like the best place for a person with "entrepreneurial spontaneity," but in retrospect he thinks being a fighter pilot suited his personality well. True, there are lots of rules on the ground, but in the air, especially in combat situations, there are no rules. Just win. It was the end that mattered, not the means. The year was now 1964, and he would soon be expected to put his training into practice.

With rumors about an upcoming deployment to Vietnam still just rumors, Nathan spent the weekend with his mother at a Christian retreat in the mountains north of Los Angeles. It was there that he met his future father-in-law. It was not Mr. B's normal practice to show young men pictures of his daughter—a student at Westmont College—but Nathan was different. He was college educated, a Navy pilot and *someone who brought his mother to a Christian retreat!* Nathan was equally impressed with the photograph of Carolyn. He responded by writing her a letter in which he revealed his love for pistachio ice cream, his love of flying the world's fastest jet (which at the time was the F-4) and his interest in possibly becoming a missionary. It is no longer clear, some forty years later, which of these attracted Carolyn the most, but the result was a three-month courtship and a wedding that had to be bumped up because of his upcoming deployment to the South China Sea.

Nathan participated in the first U.S. bombing raids over Vietnam. Altogether he flew 110 missions during his one-year tour of duty and was awarded the Air Medal for one of the first "kills" of the war—a Soviet-made MIG fighter. Between these short, adrenaline-packed "dogfights" were long, monotonous wastelands of idle time in which he would write letters home. Lots of them. He wrote Carolyn, his college writing professor and his college buddy Greg Livingstone, who was now a missionary with Operation Mobilization. He remembers, particularly in the letters to Greg, reflecting on what the status of the church must be in Indochina and speculating about his own missionary plans for the future.

After his tour of service in Vietnam he was assigned to Norfolk, Virginia, then later to Pensacola, Florida, where he was a flight school instructor. Together he and Carolyn tried to reflect Christ wherever they were. Their squeaky-clean lifestyle earned them the nicknames "Mr. and Mrs. Purex." Toward the end of his commitment to the Navy, a retired Air Force colonel dropped by for a visit. Colonel Fane, who was in town as part of that weekend's Billy Graham Crusade, had just finished talking to Bill Bright about creating a military version of the Campus Crusade ministry and wanted to talk to Nathan about helping him start it. "Come join us," he said, "and change the lives of men who are on the front lines for freedom." This became the first of a long line of ministry and business startups. Nathan resigned from the Navy in 1967 and moved to Lake Arrowhead, California.

No longer on active duty but serving in the naval reserve, Nathan began the gentle transition into civilian life. He was permitted a great deal of freedom, and he was always trying out new ideas. He eventually moved to San Diego, where, as chaplain of the Marine Corp's basic training camp, he conducted voluntary "religious education" classes with roughly fifty Marine recruits each week. These were men who expressed an interest in learning more about Christianity. Inevitably about ten to fifteen men would accept Christ each week, which served as another confirmation to Nathan that people do hunger for God, and that it's simply a matter of finding ways to help them recognize that hunger.

After ten years with Campus Crusade, Nathan left for the East Coast to attend seminary. On the side he copastored a Southern Baptist church in the Washington, D.C. area, but that relationship ended two years later because, according to Nathan, "We weren't Southern Baptist enough." While working on his doctorate, he and Carolyn started a ministry of helping local churches organize and manage their own evangelistic campaigns and were also deeply involved in other inner-city ministry activities, including planting a new church. However, when the Navy asked Nathan to return to active duty to serve as the congressional liaison, the couple jumped at the opportunity.

During all this time Nathan never lost touch with his friend Greg Livingstone and even became one of Greg's regular financial supporters. So it was not surprising when Greg called in 1983 and invited him to a Middle Eastern restaurant near Philadelphia. Greg was now the president of North Africa Mission, an organization that focused on the Arab countries of North Africa. Greg was wrestling with the challenges of a new approach for reaching Muslims. In the hundred-year history of this organization, there had been only two conversions to Christianity, and Greg was convinced they could do better. Over the next couple of hours he and Nathan talked, trying to ignore the veils of an unhappy belly dancer that were swirling in their faces. Greg and Nathan were locked in a deep discussion about new ways to bring Christ to the Muslim world. Greg concluded the discussion by challenging Nathan in a way no one had ever challenged him before: "Nathan, you've been successful in a lot of things. Now join me and together we'll be *significant* in populating the heavens with Muslim believers." Nathan recalls, "No one had ever asked me to be significant before."

Back home Carolyn was not as easily persuaded. "Just the mention of the word *Africa* almost made her faint," Nathan says. Furthermore, the family situation was the most stable it had ever been. With two small children to raise and Nathan's retirement as a Navy commander within reach, Carolyn was less attracted to the "big idea" of changing the way missions was done in the Arab world than Nathan was. Still, after much discussion and prayer, the family moved that summer to the U.S. Center for World Mission in Pasadena, California. Together Greg, Nathan and Bob Sjogren began working on what would eventually become Frontiers, a missionary sending agency focused exclusively on reaching the Muslim world for Christ.

The Muslim world presented many challenges for missionaries, not the least of which was getting missionaries *into* the country in the first place. The term *tentmaking* was only beginning to gain currency during this time, and various conflicting interpretations were floating around. Some, like Ruth Siemens of Global Opportunities, insisted the term should be applied only to lay Christians whose jobs take them to another culture, giving them a unique opportunity to integrate work and witness in places where missionaries cannot go. Others wanted to leave room for donor-supported missionaries using secular jobs as an access strategy into those "closed" countries.

Frontiers avoided the controversy altogether by not using the tentmaker label. Instead they were quite open about the fact that they were missionaries, albeit missionaries who use "creative" ways to gain access to and build relationships with Muslims. Most initially entered with tourist visas and gravitated into educational "platforms" for longer-term residency. As director of field affairs, Nathan's primary responsibilities were to coach and encourage these personnel and to help them plan long-term access strategies. "Creative access thinking" was his bent, and he was attracted primarily to the business platforms because of their independence, their flexibility and the acceptance of business in the host countries. Lots of people were willing to teach English as a second language, but those willing to take on the challenge of starting a business were rare.

Gradually, however, his "ends justify the means" way of thinking began to change. He started viewing the means as equally important. More specifically, Nathan began to advocate the idea that God cares as much about the *process* of winning people to Christ as the results. And for that matter he was just as eager to assist those who felt a calling to Hindus, Buddhists and other unreached people groups. This shift in focus, combined with his quixotic personality and military-inspired leadership style, began creating tensions within the organization.

The problems eventually came to a head in a meeting in 1987. Nathan, the board and all the team leaders gathered in Pasadena and, after a lively meeting, worked out an amicable exit. They decided to help Nathan launch a new ministry called Strategic Ventures Network (SVN), an organization that would specialize in helping missionaries who use businesses as a vehicle for reaching the least evangelized. As the leader of an independent organization, Nathan was now free to serve a wider constituency. While not a businessman himself, his experience with SVN whetted his appetite for the entrepreneurial challenge of starting and growing his own business.

His views about creative access strategies continued to evolve during this period. He began to recognize the importance of authenticity, of genuinely depending on a business for income and using it as a natural context for authentic witness. "The issue comes down to legitimacy," he argues. "If you're not profitable, you're not legitimate. And profitability demands a much higher standard of work and results than is found in many 'cover' businesses." He began articulating these views publicly, but one big problem still prevented him from being a credible voice in this area: he had no meaningful business experience himself. Thus in the early 1990s he started a company that sold phone cards internationally. But as someone who was fully supported by donors, he had little incentive to work hard at it. Finally, after deciding it was time to "quit tent-talking and begin tentmaking," Nathan began releasing his donors from their commitments in 1993 and started building Gateway Telecommunications Services (GTS).

COMPANY HISTORY

The initial reason for starting GTS was to gain business experience so that Nathan could more effectively serve others through SVN. Yet all this changed in 1997 when a declaration by the World Trade Organization (WTO) broke open the international telecommunications market. Before then, each country had its own elaborate set of regulations and restrictions that effectively kept foreign competitors out. But in 1997 the WTO deregulated the industry, or at least reduced the barriers significantly. Suddenly every kind of telecom-related service was fair game, from phone cards and call-back services to pay phones and wireless networks. Some of these markets were large, and breaking into them required extensive negotiations with the national Ministries of Communication; others were large but decentralized, providing many opportunities to carve out small but profitable niches.

The company's first two efforts flopped. One was to sell long-distance services (with the help of a national telecom partner) to mission and ministry organizations. The promise of profits being used to fund kingdom work was not enough to get more than a few customers to make the switch. Another effort—selling phone cards and "call back" services in Argentina—showed great promise initially, but the low entry barriers and cut-throat competition quickly made it impossible to build the effort into a sustainable business. Nevertheless, GTS gradually began to find defendable niches, particularly in the area of meeting the telecom needs of tourists. Furthermore, Nathan began to recruit and train sales agents, some tentmaker-missionaries, some Christian nationals and some non-Christians, and together they all began "learning the ropes" about how to succeed in these markets.

GTS was finally showing some promise, but it was clear that long-run success would require more capital. So Nathan and Carolyn mortgaged their home and poured the money into the company. Their son, Darick, sensing that his parents were in way over their head, at least in terms of the technological skills needed to grow the business, turned down an offer to become a state trooper (his dream job) and joined the management team of GTS.

Like many startups, GTS grew in fits and starts. There were times when it seemed they would lose everything, including their home. But they persisted and grew GTS into a small but respectable—and profitable—company. Perhaps the most challenging part of growing the company was finding sales agents among believers, both missionaries and nationals, who understood what Nathan was trying to do. At first he thought it would be easy: "I thought I could just let the word out that I'm looking for tentmakers, and they would come running." Well, they came running, but he quickly learned that "our starting points were different, they just *seemed* the same." They were both talking about the opportunity this gave families to live in a "creative access country" with the help of a GTS visa. What was not obvious to the prospective agents was that Nathan was advocating a new idea. "We viewed it as a legitimate, full-on business, with all the hard work that implies."

Sadly, while selling an attractive new service to hotels and telecoms may have sounded easy at first, not many were interested in putting in the hard work necessary to translate ideas into success. Most had little, if any, experience in business, some having never worked in a performance-based job after college or seminary. Even the nationals, who were picked for their roles in the national church (usually a threatened minority), seemed to treat business as a distraction unless it was convenient and involved little effort. Of course Nathan must assume at least some responsibility for these misunderstandings, given his own history in promoting businesses as access strategies. Moreover, regarding both his terminology (tentmakers, creative access and so on) and his audience (missionary sending agencies), it was natural for them to misunderstand the purpose of the company. In the end, recruitment and training was a long, trial-and-error process that consumed much more of Nathan's energies than he had anticipated, which left Darick principally in charge of the day-to-day management of the company.

By 1997 GTS had nineteen sales agents in fifteen countries. Eleven of them were various shades of tentmaker-missionaries and kingdom professionals. Though still relatively small, the company had become one of the most successful and aggressive players in the niche market they were competing in. But it was time for another infusion of capital. Nathan updated the business plan and began the arduous task of raising outside capital. Some Christians nibbled but did not invest. In mid-1998 a pair of New Zealander nonbelievers with extensive experience in the industry entered into serious talks with Nathan and Darick about forming a new jointly owned company. But those talks broke down in the late stages over disagreement on issues related to the ownership and control of the company.

As a result of the yearlong strains related to raising capital and the failed merger talks, Darick and Nathan decided it was time to sell the company. Shortly before Christmas, however, Darick was diagnosed with terminal cancer. During the next six months, Nathan juggled the sale of the company and the closing of some telecom contracts in Southeast Asia and Australia, all while also tending to his son and his son's family. Obviously it was a difficult period. In May 1999, less than six months after the initial diagnosis, Darick was gone, and the company was in the final stages of escrow.

THE MINISTRY STORY

Nathan's views about using business merely as an "access strategy" for missionaries evolved considerably over the years. When he founded GTS he viewed business as an important part of the process, but was open to allowing some hybrid tentmaker-missionaries to "work" for his company. By the time he sold the company he was an outspoken critic of missionaries who wear business disguises, even though some remained affiliated with his company. This presented Nathan with a moral dilemma when the decision was made to sell the company: sell to the highest bidder even though that would likely result in the termination of those underperforming sales agents, or accept a lower bid from a sympathetic buyer?

In the end, Nathan sold the company to a like-minded Christian who pledged to preserve Nathan's vision of integrating business and missions. In return, Nathan agreed to help finance the sale of the company and to remain an active adviser. Thus we can say with confidence that the company's missional impact is similar now to what it was under Nathan's leadership. That impact can be divided into two pieces: the personal relationships Nathan has built with his agents and customers, and the impact his agents are having in their specific contexts.

From Nathan's perspective, the most rewarding part of owning a GCC is facilitating the ministry of others. While some of his agents did not meet his expectations for the business, most are seeing the tremendous ministry potential that results from integrating work and witness. Put another way, they are seeing a direct correlation between their accomplishments at work and the ability to have an impact in other people's lives. For example, the commissions earned by one agent in South Asia (a citizen of that country) make it possible for him not only to provide full employment for three men whom he has been discipling but also to use half his income to support a local orphanage. A new church has been planted, thanks in part to the opportunity the company provided this agent to have an authentic workplace context from which to build relationships. One formerly donor-supported missionary jumped at the opportunity to work for GTS, saying he had become discouraged by the questions that are inevitably raised when a person appears to be "hanging around" with little legitimate commercial identity and no obvious source of income. Today he is not only discipling his coworkers in the faith but also mentoring them in the business, including turning some of his biggest accounts over to otherwise unemployable converts. Other agents have expressed relief that they do not have to do what Nathan calls "low level import/export stuff," but instead can be viewed in the eyes of the locals as "real" business people.

All told, the company is an important source of income for national

Christians in Cyprus, Uruguay, Romania, Poland, Sweden and New Zealand. In addition, it provides a context for workplace-based ministry for expatriates in Turkey, India, three Arab Gulf countries, China, Israel, Morocco and Spain.

ANALYSIS AND CONCLUSIONS

GTS is—or at least was—more loose-knit and decentralized than any of the other companies profiled in this book. The business model is low-cost and extremely flexible. Because of the nature of the business, this model suits the company well. In fact, earlier in the book we suggested that Cedric's business model might end up resembling Nathan's in many ways. However, as a GCC, the company was a bit too loose-knit for our taste. There was little reporting or accountability necessary from the agents and no one to whom Nathan was formally accountable. Some would say that this is as it should be; after all, it was his money and home that were on the line. This is true, and many entrepreneurs are naturally wary about anything that limits their flexibility and ability to make decisions, especially when they are the ones with the most to lose. But in terms of the ministry impact, because there were no goals and no reporting requirements, it is impossible to say how well the company did. Missions audits, business audits and communicating with the various stakeholders—all appropriate functions of a board of directors—were not built into the GTS model. We feel that the company's overall effectiveness suffered as a result of its failure to have even so much as an advisory board.

We must remember, however, that this was Nathan's first attempt at launching a GCC, and no one profiled in this book has done it perfectly. Indeed this is a new idea for everyone and there are still many things that need to be worked out in terms of our methods and motives. As we transition from one missions paradigm to another, there will be a need for much more theological reflection about some of the issues raised in this case, as well as a need for more people like Nathan to put everything on the line for the sake of trying new ideas. Even as we speak, Nathan is at it again, this time building on the successes and limitations of his earlier effort—including accountability, transferability and advisory assistance.

QUESTIONS FOR REVIEW

1. What were the important stages of Nathan's preparation? In retrospect, what could he have done better?

2. What training, experience and qualifications would you look for in prospective sales agents for a company like this?

3. If you were evaluating GTS according to the questions in the sidebar "Assessing the Viability of a GCC" (pp. 94-95), how would it measure up? What are its principle strengths and weaknesses?

4. Do you agree or disagree with Nathan's views about tentmaking and using business as an entry strategy? Please explain.

5. In terms of success and effectiveness, how does this company compare with the others profiled in the book?

12

CONCLUSION

Christians today earn about one-quarter of all the income in the world. Thus, any effort to correct the ills of our current system must begin with a look at how we acquire this income and how we use it. . . . Unfortunately, you could go to many churches for a month of Sundays and not hear this message of stewardship. More than likely you would hear the principle of stewardship limited to a call to put more in the offering plate.

LARRY REED

There once was a time when the simple act of sending money to missionaries gave people at home an adequate sense of connectedness and participation. Today that same act often connotes a *disconnectedness*, as the participation essentially ends for most donors when their check enters the offering plate. We believe that the trends in church giving toward more local, visible ministries reflects a desire to *see* and participate more directly in the ministry of the church. Christians are not losing interest in the poorest and the least reached so much as they are failing to see a connection between their current circumstances and those of people in other parts of the world. There are countless people, like John Sage of Pura Vida Coffee, who are yearning to find ways to combine their passions for business and ministry but are hearing from the pulpits that they must change careers and go into traditional ministry in order to "finish well." This is unfortunate because there is potentially no limit to the resources—human and financial—that will be unleashed once business professionals see the connection between their gifts, their *current* occupation and the mission of the church.

In chapters seven through eleven we profiled just a few of the ways business professionals are becoming more directly involved in that mission. What they show is a missions paradigm in transition and all the ambiguities that go along with such a transition. While many people support the idea of integrating business and missions, significant differences of opinion remain as to what that should look like in practice. Some believe it is possible and entirely appropriate to expect kingdom professionals to be effective crosscultural witnesses for Christ. Others expect less crosscultural witness from kingdom professionals and are more open to integrating missionaries into the business to fill critical gaps. Some believe kingdom professionals, particularly westerners, should stay home altogether and apply themselves instead toward creating wealth and transferring it to indigenous missionary or business efforts.

What we hope we have shown is that the "correct" answer depends on the circumstances. Certainly a top priority should be given to partnering with the indigenous churches in their efforts to usher in social, economic and spiritual transformation. Bringing a foreign-owned GCC into the community can be perfectly consistent with that goal, although there are other things kingdom professionals can do as well. For example, the Business Professional Network (BPN) assists Christian entrepreneurs in the developing world by linking them with "business development groups" in the West. These are church-based groups of business professionals who create and manage a revolving fund for small- and medium-size enterprises (SMEs). BPN provides assistance when necessary, particularly in the early stages, but all organizational and decision-making responsibilities rest with the group. (Visit <www.bpn.org > for more information.) Evangelistic Commerce (EC) is another organization that seeks to link resources in the West—in this case Christian-owned companies—with missionary efforts in the developing world. (Visit <www.evangelisticcommerce.org> for more information.) An excellent way to learn more about these and other ways to get more involved is to attend one of the seminars or vision trips that are organized by both EC and BPN.

NEXT STEPS

One reason our case studies focused more on the people behind the business than the business itself is because, after spending years comparing and contrasting GCCs, we have found that without question the most important determinant of a GCC's success and effectiveness is the people. Indeed, some of the most successful GCCs have been started by people with no prior business experience or training. How then can we call them kingdom professionals? The answer is simple: these people recognized from day one the importance of doing things right, learning the necessary skills when possible and bringing others onto the team to fill critical gaps. This is in fact what all successful business professionals do.

Our research also uncovered other common themes.

- No business is perfect and mistakes will be made, especially early on.

- The most effective GCCs are those that are managed by *teams* of kingdom professionals, ideally multicultural teams that include local believers.

- The most effective GCCs work in formal or informal partnership with established churches, ministries and agencies.

- The most successful and effective GCCs are those that are treated as real businesses, with all the accompanying expectations of excellence and professionalism.

- The most effective kingdom professionals are those who have a long history of active involvement in ministry and missions even before starting a GCC. Furthermore, while not neglecting near-culture outreach, their passion for seeing more distant cultures reached with the gospel grows over time.

- The most effective kingdom professionals have an integrated view of work, business and ministry, and they are comfortable with their calling as bearers of good news in and through the marketplace.

- Fierce spiritual opposition is a certainty, and accountability at the individual and corporate level is essential.

How does one prepare for this kind of ministry? First we should note that every one of the novice-turned-kingdom-professionals profiled in this book—Jeff Nolan, Craig Stewart and Nathan Jenkins—agree that if they had it to do over again, they would get the appropriate business training and experience before embarking on this journey. Indeed, as we saw with John Larson and John Sage, the experience gained in a secular context is often a central part of the equipping process. It should never be viewed as a "necessary evil" but rather as "today's assignment" by a God who is both using us now and preparing us for future service. That preparation may include twenty years or four years of faithfully reflecting Christ in corporate America. It may include three graduate degrees or none. You get the point.

The most effective kingdom professionals—whether working in a pioneering or facilitative context—also demonstrate some level of competence in the areas of crosscultural communication, cultural anthropology, foreign language acquisition, church planting and spiritual warfare. Many get this through formal training. Others, like John Larson, take a less formal but nevertheless very deliberate approach to acquiring the necessary skills. Either way, all aspiring kingdom professionals should seek to improve these skills because reflecting Christ crossculturally requires significant changes in a person's perspective.

It is encouraging to see that some business programs, like Biola's, are starting to create degree programs for those specifically interested in reflecting Christ crossculturally. Likewise, some seminaries and schools of world mission—like those at Fuller, Gordon-Conwell and Regent College—are beginning to offer seminars, conferences and certificate programs that focus on the role of business in the mission of the church. We expect these trends to continue because globalization is causing business to become an increasingly important part of the mission of the church. GCCs represent a return to a much older paradigm, one that places laypeople who are living out their faith in a secular workplace environment squarely in the middle of the missionary enterprise. Those sitting in the stands are now being thrust into the game, sometimes without adequate training or experience. It is therefore appropriate that universities, churches and mission agencies take a fresh look at how to better equip laypeople and what should be expected from them. We trust that this book has shed some light on those questions.

APPENDIX

GOING DEEPER:
SELECTED RESOURCES FOR FURTHER RESEARCH

BOOKS

Banks, Robert, and Julia Banks. *The Church Comes Home: A New Base for Community and Mission*. Peabody, Mass.: Hendrickson, 1998.

Befus, David R. *Kingdom Business: The Ministry of Promoting Economic Development*. Miami: Latin America Mission, 2002. Available at <www.lam.org>.

Burkett, Larry. *Business by the Book: The Complete Guide of Biblical Principles for the Workplace*. Nashville: Thomas Nelson, 1998.

Danker, William. *Profit for the Lord*. Grand Rapids: Eerdmans, 1971. Available at <www.intent.org>.

Elmer, Duane. *Cross-Cultural Connections: Stepping Out and Fitting In Around the World*. Downers Grove, Ill.: InterVarsity Press, 2002.

Gudykunst, William B., Stellat Ting-Toomey and Tsukasa Nishida, eds. *Communication in Personal Relationships Across Cultures*. Thousand Oaks, Calif.: SAGE, 1996.

Hammond, Pete, R. Paul Stevens and Todd Svanoe. *The Marketplace Annotated Bibliography*. Downers Grove, Ill.: InterVarsity Press, 2002.

Lingenfelter, Sherwood G., and Marvin K. Mayers. *Ministering Cross-Culturally: An Incarnational Model for Personal Relationships*. Grand Rapids: Baker, 1986.

Myers, Bryant. *Walking with the Poor: Principles and Practices of Tranformational Development*. Maryknoll, N.Y.: Orbis, 1999.

Patterson, George, and Richard Scoggins. *Church Multiplication Guide: Helping Churches to Reproduce Locally and Abroad*. Pasadena, Calif.: William Carey Library, 1993.

Sherman, Doug, and William Hendricks. *Your Work Matters to God.* Colorado Springs: NavPress, 1987.

Silvoso, Ed. *Anointed for Business: How Christians Can Use Their Influence in the Marketplace to Change the World.* Ventura, Calif.: Regal, 2002.

———. *That None Should Perish: How to Reach Entire Cities for Christ Through Prayer Evangelism.* Ventura, Calif.: Regal, 1994.

Steffen, Tom. *Reconnecting God's Story to Ministry: Crosscultural Storytelling at Home and Abroad.* La Habra, Calif.: Center for Organizational & Ministry Development, 1996.

———. *Passing the Baton: Church Planting That Empowers.* Rev. ed. La Habra, Calif.: Center for Organizational & Ministry Development, 1997).

Stevens, Paul. *The Other Six Days: Vocation, Work, and Ministry in Biblical Perspective.* Grand Rapids: Eerdmans, 1999.

Yamamori, Tetsunao, and Ken Eldred, eds. *On Kingdom Business: Transforming World Mission Through Kingdom Entrepreneurship.* Wheaton, Ill.: Crossway, 2003.

OTHER USEFUL RESOURCES

Caleb Project: <www.calebproject.org>

Centre for Entrepreneurship & Economic Development:
   <www.ceed-uofn.org>

CIA World Factbook: <www.cia.gov/cia/publications/factbook/>
   Some people may be surprised to learn that the CIA collects and makes available to the public some of the most comprehensive country-specific data on demographics, infrastructure, geography and economic conditions.

Connecting Business Men to Christ (CBMC): <www.cbmc.com>

Country Commercial Guides (CCGs): <www.usatrade.gov/website/ccg.nsf>
   These country-specific guides are updated annually and contain reports on economic trends, trade regulations, political environment, and much more.

Fellowship of Companies for Christ: <www.fcci.org>

Global Mapping International: <www.gmi.org>

Global Opportunities: <www.globalopps.org>

Human Development Reports: <http://hdr.undp.org/reports/default.cfm>

Intent: <www.intent.org>

InterVarsity Christian Fellowship's MBA Ministry: <www.intervarsity.org/grad/mba/index.html>

Joshua Project II: <www.joshuaproject.net>

National Trade Data Bank: <www.stat-usa.gov/ntdb>

Some of the information available at this site is available for a fee, but there is also much that can be accessed for free, such as the International Marketing Insight (IMI) Reports, Industry Sector Analysis (ISA) Reports, and Best Market Reports.

PeopleTeams.org: <www.peopleteams.org>

Scruples: <www.scruples.org>

NOTES

Chapter 1: The Good News About Globalization

[1]R. Paul Stevens, *The Other Six Days: Vocation, Work, and Ministry in Biblical Perspective* (Grand Rapids: Eerdmans, 1999), p. 208.

[2]Ed Silvoso, *Anointed for Business: How Christians Can Use Their Influence in the Marketplace to Change the World* (Ventura, Calif.: Regal, 2002), p. 24.

[3]David B. Barrett, George T. Kurian and Todd M. Johnson, eds., *World Christian Encyclopedia: A Comparative Survey of Churches and Religions in the Modern World* (New York: Oxford University Press, 2001), 1:360.

[4]C. Neal Johnson, "Toward a Marketplace Missiology," *Missiology: An International Review* 31, no. 1 (2003): 87-97.

[5]David English, "Paul's Secret: A 1st-Century Strategy for a 21st-Century World," *World Christian* 14, no. 3 (2001): 22-26.

[6]Edmund Oliver, *The Social Achievements of the Christian Church* (Board of Evangelism and Social Service of the United Church of Canada, 1930), pp. 67-68.

[7]See, for example, William Danker, *Profit for the Lord* (Grand Rapids: Eerdmans, 1971); and Vishal Mangalwadi and Ruth Mangalwadi, *The Legacy of William Carey* (Wheaton, Ill.: Good News Publishers, 1999).

[8]Michael McLoughlin, "Back to the Future of Missions: The Case for Marketplace Ministry," *Vocatio,* December 2000, pp. 1-6.

[9]Quoted in McLoughlin, "Back to the Future," p. 3.

[10]David Van Biema, "Missionaries Undercover," *Time,* June 30, 2003, pp. 36-44.

[11]John J. Goldman, "Ex-Army Sergeant Admits Guilt in '98 Embassy Blasts," *Los Angeles Times,* October 21, 2000; and John J. Goldman, "Accused Bomber Was Businessman, Not Terrorist, Defense Lawyer Says" *Los Angeles Times*, May 4, 2001.

[12]Dina Kraft, "Israelis Help Engineer Rich's Pardon Campaign," available at <www.freep.com/backindex/2001/02/16/newsindex.htm>.

[13]Terry McDermott and Soraya Sarhaddi Nelson, "7 Accused of Raising Funds at Airports for Iran Terrorist Group," *Los Angeles Times,* March 1, 2001.

[14]See the statement by the Consultation on Mission Language and Metaphors at <http://globalmission.org/canada/articles/mission_language.htm>. Also see Richard Beaton, "New Testament Metaphors and the Christian Mission," *Evangelical Missions Quarterly* 37, no. 1 (2001): 60-64; and Rick Love, "Muslims and Military Metaphors," *Evangelical Missions Quarterly* 37, no. 1 (2001): 65-68.

Chapter 2: Toward a Definition of a Great Commission Company

[1]Andreas Köstenberger and Peter O'Brien, *Salvation to the Ends of the Earth: A Biblical Theology of Mission* (Downers Grove, Ill.: InterVarsity Press, 2001), p. 26.

[2]Ibid., p. 27.

[3]Bryant Myers, *Walking with the Poor: Principles and Practices of Transformational Development* (Maryknoll, N.Y.: Orbis, 1999), p. 27.

[4]David Bosch, *Transforming Mission: Paradigm Shifts in Theology of Mission* (Maryknoll, N.Y.: Orbis, 1991), p. 9.

[5]Andrew Kirk, *What Is Mission? Theological Explorations* (Minneapolis: Fortress, 2000), p. 30.

[6]Bong R. Ro, "The Perspectives of Church History from New Testament Times to 1960" in *In Word and Deed: Evangelism and Social Responsibility,* ed. Bruce J. Nicholls (Grand Rapids: Eerdmans, 1985), p. 17.

[7]Ralph Winter, "From Mission to Evangelism to Mission," *International Journal of Frontier Missions* 19, no. 4 (2002): 6-8.

[8]Dallas Willard, *The Divine Conspiracy: Rediscovering Our Hidden Life in God* (San Francisco: HarperSanFrancisco, 1998), p. 12.

[9]Myers, *Walking with the Poor,* p. 6.

[10]A published version of the initial stage of this dialogue can be found in *Faith in Development: Partnership between the World Bank and the Churches of Africa* (Oxford: Regnum Books, 2001). The World Bank describes the dialogue and subsequent book as one that "presents development issues within a church context and provides insight into *the spiritual dimension of poverty"* (emphasis added).

[11]From the Thailand Statement of the Consultation on World Evangelization, Pattaya, Thailand, June 16-27, 1980. Cited in John Stott, *Making Christ Known* (Grand Rapids: Eerdmans, 1996).

[12]Myers, *Walking with the Poor,* p. 39 (emphasis added).

[13]Gary Ginter, "Overcoming Resistance Through Tentmaking," in *Reaching the Resistant: Barriers and Bridges for Mission,* EMS Series, ed. J. Dudley Woodberry (Pasadena, Calif.: William Carey Library, 1998), 6:209-18.

[14]Gary Ginter, "Kingdom Professionals: An Old Idea in New Wineskins," *Paraclete Perspectives* 1, no. 2 (2002): 1, 8.

[15]For more elaboration on this point, see David English, "Paul's Secret: A 1st-Century Strategy for a 21st-Century World," *World Christian* 14, no. 3 (2001): 22-26; and Ruth E. Siemens, "Why Did Paul Make Tents? A Biblical Basis for Tentmaking," *GO Paper* A-1 (1998). Both articles are available at <www.globalopps.org/materials.htm>.

[16]Kirk, *What Is Mission?* p. 73.

[17]Ibid.

[18]William Pollard, quoted in Marc Gunther, "God and Business," *Fortune,* July 9, 2001, pp. 59-80.

[19]Gary Ginter, personal communication, May 29, 2003.

Chapter 3: Globalization and Business

[1]See, for example, Oswald Firth, "Globalization: A Christian Perspective on Economics," *Dialogue Columbo* 24 (1997): 101-34.

[2]World Bank, *Global Economic Prospects and the Developing Countries* (Washington, D.C.: The World Bank, 2003), p. 30.

[3]Michael Mussa, "Factors Driving Global Economic Integration," in *Global Economic Integra-*

tion: Opportunities and Challenges (Federal Reserve Bank of Kansas City, 2000). Also available at <http://www.kc.frb.org/publicat/sympos/2000/sym00prg.htm>.

[4]United Nations Development Programme, *Human Development Report 2001* (New York: Oxford University Press, 2001).

[5]See, for example, Paul Cleveland et al., *A Catholic Response to Economic Globalization: Applications of Catholic Social Teaching,* Christian Social Thought Series (Grand Rapids: Center of Economic Personalism, 2001), p. 1.

[6]Pope John Paul II, "Jubilee Implies Commitment to Justice, Address to Centesimus-Pro Pontifice," *L'Osservatore Romano,* September 22, 1999, p. 6.

[7]World Trade Organization, Press Pack (Nov. 28, 1999), p. 63. Available at <www.wto.org/english/thewto_e/minist_e/min99_e/english/about_e/presspack_english.pdf>.

[8]UNCTAD, *World Investment Report 2002* (New York: United Nations), pp. xv, 2.

[9]UNCTAD, *World Investment Report 1999* (New York: United Nations), p. 4.

[10]Derived from UNCTAD, *World Investment Report 2002* (New York: United Nations), table I.1, and the WTO, *International Trade Statistics 2002* (New York: World Trade Organization), table II.1.

[11]Kenichi Ohmae, *The Borderless World: Power and Strategy in the Interlinked Economy,* rev. ed. (New York: HarperCollins, 1999), pp. 9-10.

[12]"One World?" *The Economist,* October 18, 1997, p. 80.

[13]Jeffrey Frankel, "Globalization of the Economy," Working Paper 7858, National Bureau of Economic Research, August 2000, p. 2.

[14]UNCTAD, *World Investment Report 1999,* p. xxiv.

[15]UNCTAD, *World Investment Report 2002,* table I.2.1.

[16]Thomas Friedman, *The Lexus and the Olive Tree,* 2nd ed. (New York: Anchor Books, 2000), p. 162.

[17]Andrew Kirk, *What Is Mission? Theological Explorations.* (Minneapolis: Fortress, 2000), p. 24.

[18]UNCTAD, *World Investment Report 1999,* derived from calculations based on data in annex table B.1.

[19]Ibid., derived from annex table B.2.

[20]M. W. Peng and P. S. Heath, "The Growth of the Firm in Planned Economies in Transition: Institutions, Organizations, and Strategic Choice," *Academy of Management Review* 21, no. 2 (1996): 3.

[21]See the studies cited in J. S. Black and M. Mendenhall, "Cross Cultural Training Effectiveness: A Review and a Theoretical Framework for Future Research," *Academy of Management Review,* 15, no. 1 (1990): 113-16. Also Susan McGrath-Champ, Xiaohua Yang and Georgia Chao, "Effects of Expatriate Training on Firm Performance: A Conceptual Approach" (paper presented at the meetings of the Academy of International Business, Sydney, Australia, November 16-19, 2001).

[22]See Theodore H. Moran, *Beyond Sweatshops: Foreign Direct Investment and Globalization in Developing Countries* (Washington, D.C.: Brookings Institution Press, 2002) for a fascinating and detailed look at how these policies actually undermine economic development.

[23]Hans Christiansen, *Foreign Direct Investment for Development: Maximising Benefits, Minimising Costs* (Paris: Organization for Economic Cooperation and Development, 2002), pp. 16-17.

Chapter 4: Globalization and Missions

[1]David B. Barrett, George T. Kurian and Todd M. Johnson, eds., *World Christian Encyclopedia: A Comparative Survey of Churches and Religions in the Modern World* (New York: Oxford University Press, 2001), 2:660.

[2]Barrett, Kurian and Johnson, *World Christian Encyclopedia,* table 1.3.

[3]Ralph D. Winter, "The New Macedonia: A Revolutionary New Era in Mission Begins," in *Perspectives on the World Christian Movement,* ed. R. D. Winter and S. C. Hawthorne, 3rd ed. (Pasadena, Calif.: William Carey Library, 1999), pp. 339-53.

[4]Tom Sine, *Mustard Seed Versus McWorld: Reinventing Christian Life and Mission for a New Millennium* (Grand Rapids: Baker, 1999), chap. six.

[5]Interdev, quoted in Sine, *Mustard Seed,* p. 126.

[6]Joshua Project II <http://www.joshuaproject.net/definitions.html>.

[7]Joshua Project II <http://www.joshuaproject.net/introleastreached.html >.

[8]Lant Pritchett, "Divergence, Big Time," *Journal of Economic Perspectives* (Summer 1997): 3-17.

[9]History has shown that this problem very often leads either to revolution or to government repression. What this would look like on a global scale is a subject we will leave for those with a penchant for end-times prophecy.

[10]John Hanford, quoted in Stan Guthrie, *Missions in the Third Millennium: 21 Key Trends for the 21st Century* (Waynesboro, Ga.: Paternoster, 2000), p. 182.

[11]David Barrett, "Status of Global Mission, 1996," *International Bulletin of Missionary Research* 20, no. 1 (1996): 25.

[12]Paul Marshall, *Religious Freedom in the World: A Global Report on Freedom and Persecution* (Nashville: Broadman & Holman, 2000).

[13]C. K. Prahalad and Stuart L. Hart, "The Fortune at the Bottom of the Pyramid," *Strategy and Business* 26, no. 1 (2002): 55-67; and C. K. Prahalad and Allen Hammond, "Serving the World's Poor, Profitably" *Harvard Business Review,* September 2002, pp. 48-57.

[14]See, for example, the fascinating collection of essays in Lawrence E. Harrison and Samuel P. Huntington, *Culture Matters: How Values Shape Human Progress* (New York: Basic Books, 2000); and the essay by Luigi Guiso, Paola Sapienza and Luigi Zingales, "People's Opium? Religion and Economic Attitudes," *NBER Working Paper #w9237,* September 2002.

[15]Elizabeth Brusco, *The Reformation of Machismo: Evangelical Conversion and Gender in Columbia* (Austin, Tex.: University of Texas Press, 1995).

[16]Amy Sherman, *The Soul of Development: Biblical Christianity and Economic Transformation in Guatemala* (New York: Oxford University Press, 1997), pp. 163-64.

Chapter 5: Turning Vision into Action

[1]Amar Bhide, "How Entrepreneurs Craft Strategies that Work," *Harvard Business Review,* March/April 1994, pp. 150-61.

[2]Ian C. Macmillan, "The Politics of New Venture Management," in *The Entrepreneurial Venture,* ed. William Sahlman and Howard Stevenson (Boston: Harvard Business School Publications, 1992), pp. 160-68.

[3]William A. Sahlman, "How to Write a Great Business Plan," *Harvard Business Review,* July/August 1997, pp. 98-108.

[4]Ibid., p. 99.
[5]Ibid., p. 100.

Chapter 6: Sustaining Success

[1]The law allows tax-exempt nonprofits to make "prudent investments," including ownership of profit-making businesses, depending on the size of the nonprofit. Furthermore, the missional purpose of a GCC can make such ownership stakes easier to justify. However, a GCC that is part owned by a mission agency will send mixed signals, so a better approach might be to assign that ownership stake to an individual representing the agency rather than to the agency itself.

Chapter 7: The Independent, Pioneering GCC: Silk Road Handicraft Company

[1]Sadly this kind of contract often leads to sweatshop situations, because there are few, if any, penalties imposed for abuses.
[2]See, for example, Ed Silvoso, *That None Should Perish: How to Reach Entire Cities for Christ Through Prayer Evangelism* (Venture, Calif.: Gospel Light, 1997).

Chapter 9: The Facilitative Alliance: Pura Vida Coffee

[1]Some parts of this section draw heavily from the company's Private Placement Memorandum.

Chapter 10: The Pioneering Alliance: Global Engineering and Management Solutions

[1]Throughout the rest of this book the term "tentmaker-missionary" will refer to those who attempt to maintain a secular identity in their adopted country but who are identified as missionaries at home, affiliated with a missionary sending agency and supported by donations made to that agency.